MECHANICS: AN EASY APPROACH

Mechanics: An Easy Approach

For Undergraduate and Postgraduate Physics Students

by

Bikash Kumar Naik

Notion Press

This book, *Mechanics: An Easy Approach*, with its subtitle *For Undergraduate and Postgraduate Physics Students* , is a comprehensive guide to Mechanics for Undergraduate and Postgraduate Physics Students. The content is based on the latest CBCS NEP-2020 syllabus and is intended for educational purposes only. Any resemblance to actual textbooks, publishers, or other works is purely coincidental.

First edition, 2024

Published by Notion Press

Preface

MECHANICS forms the cornerstone of physics, providing fundamental principles that underpin a wide array of natural phenomena and technological applications. This book, Mechanics for Undergraduate and Postgraduate Physics Students, is meticulously designed to align with the latest Choice-Based Credit System (CBCS) and National Education Policy (NEP-2020) syllabus. It aims to serve as a comprehensive resource for students embarking on their journey to understand the intricacies of mechanics.

The content in this book is presented with clarity and rigor, emphasizing conceptual understanding and practical applications. Special care has been taken to bridge the gap between theory and real-world problems, ensuring that students can appreciate the relevance of mechanics in scientific advancements and everyday experiences. Each chapter includes detailed explanations, illustrative examples, and problem sets tailored to reinforce the learning objectives outlined in the curriculum.

The adoption of NEP-2020 heralds a paradigm shift in education, fostering multidisciplinary learning and critical thinking. This book reflects those ideals by integrating problem-solving strategies, analytical techniques, and insights into modern research trends in mechanics. By doing so, it equips students not only to excel academically but also to contribute meaningfully to the ever-evolving field of physics.

I am grateful to educators, colleagues, and students whose feedback and support have been invaluable in shaping this text. I hope this book inspires curiosity and nurtures a deeper appreciation for the elegance and utility of mechanics.

Bikash Kumar Naik

Layout of mechanics course

- Mathematical concepts of partial differentiation and coordinate systems.

- Constraints, degree's of freedom and generalized coordinates.

- Challenges with unknown nature of constrain forces in Newtonian Mechanics

- D'Alembert's Principle of virtual work to remove the constrain forces from analysis.

- Lagrange's equation: An alternative to Newton's law

- Variational method and Lagrange's equation from variational principle

- Hamiltonian equations of motion

Analytical mechanics

**Introduction of new concepts of mechanics
beyond Newton's law:
Largangian and Hamiltonian equations**

Why this is important?

❏ Making the analysis easier, in particular complex dynamical situations with imposed constrains/conditions.

❏ More general concepts extendable to other modern area of physics like quantum mechanics, field theory etc.

Review of certain mathematical concepts

Key to understand classical mechanics

Total Differential: Function of one variable

$y = f(x)$ *is a function of one variable x*

$$f'(x) = \frac{dy}{dx} = \underset{\Delta x \to 0}{Lt} \frac{\Delta y}{\Delta x} = \underset{\Delta x \to 0}{Lt} \frac{f(x + \Delta x) - f(x)}{\Delta x}$$

$$dy = [f'(x)]\, dx$$

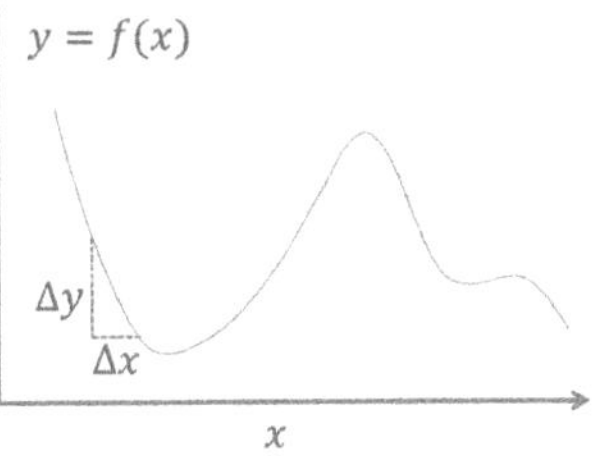

- Infinitesimal change of y around certain point (x) =(rate of change of y around the point) (magnitude of change in x)

- At stationary points (A,B, C), y does not changes $[dy = 0]$ even if x is changed infinitesimally,
which implies that at those points $f'(x) = 0$.

Partial differential: function of more than one variables

$f(x, y)$ depends on two independent variables x and y.

Example: Height (f) of a hill as function of position coordinate (x, y).

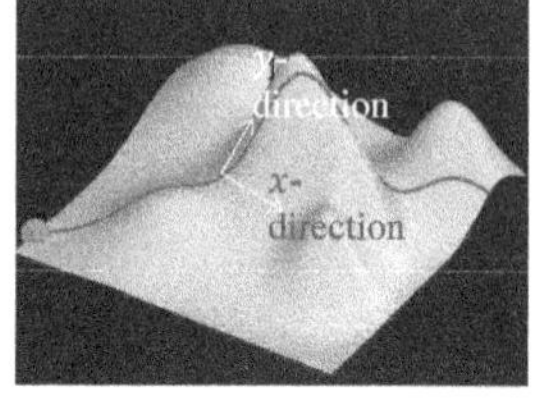

❑ The rate of change (slope) in the $'x'\,direction$, when y remains constant is denoted by

$$(\frac{\partial f}{\partial x})_y = \underset{\Delta x \to 0}{Lt} \frac{f(x + \Delta x, y) - f(x, y)}{\Delta x}$$

❑ The rate of change in the $'y'\,direction$, when x remains constant is denoted by

$$(\frac{\partial f}{\partial y})_x = \underset{\Delta y \to 0}{Lt} \frac{f(x, y + \Delta y) - f(x, y)}{\Delta y}$$

Partial differential

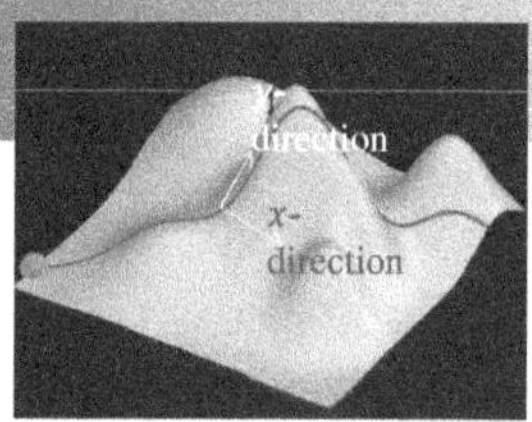

- **Change in height if I walk in the 'x' direction** [keeping 'y' fixed] **by 'dx' ?**

$$[df]_{dx} = (\frac{\partial f}{\partial x})dx$$

$$= (rate\ of\ change\ in\ 'x'\ direction)(\ amount\ of\ change\ in\ x)$$

- Similarly, $[df]_{dy} = (\frac{\partial f}{\partial y})dy$

Partial differential

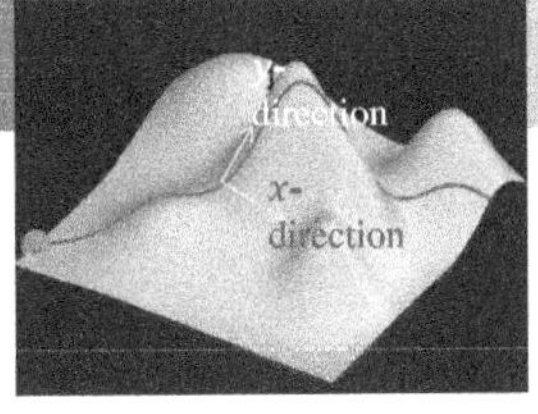

Change in height if I go in the arbitrary direction so that 'x' changes by 'dx' and 'y' also changes by 'dy'

$$df = \left(\frac{\partial f}{\partial x}\right)dx + \left(\frac{\partial f}{\partial y}\right)dy \qquad = [df]_{dx} + [df]_{dy}$$

- Generalization for a function which depends on several variables $f(x_1, x_2, x_3 \dots x_n)$

$$df = \left(\frac{\partial f}{\partial x_1}\right)dx_1 + \left(\frac{\partial f}{\partial x_2}\right)dx_2 + \dots + \left(\frac{\partial f}{\partial x_n}\right)dx_n = \sum \left(\frac{\partial f}{\partial x_i}\right)dx_i$$

Partial differential (Examples)

- $f(x,y) = a\,x^2 + b\,y^2$

$$\frac{\partial f}{\partial x} = 2\,a\,x \qquad\qquad \frac{\partial f}{\partial y} = 2\,b\,y$$

- $f(x,y) = a\,x^2 y + b$

$$\frac{\partial f}{\partial x} = 2\,a\,x\,y \qquad\qquad \frac{\partial f}{\partial y} = ax2$$

- $f(x,\theta) = a\,x\,\mathrm{Sin}(\theta) + b\,\theta^2$

$$\frac{\partial f}{\partial x} = a\,\mathbf{Sin}(\theta) \qquad \frac{\partial f}{\partial \theta} = a\,x\,\mathrm{Cos}(\theta) + 2b\,\theta$$

$f(x, y)$ is such that x and y are function of another variable say, u. We wish to find the derivative $\frac{df}{du}$.

Example: $f = xy + \ln y^2$

(we say, f depends x & y explicitly;
f depends u implicitly!)

Let, $x = a \cos u$ and $y = a \sin u$

How to calculate $\frac{df}{du}$?

Method 1: Direct substitution

Step 1: $f = (a \cos u)(a \sin u) + \ln(a \sin u)^2$

Step 2: Find $\frac{df}{du}$

Distance of the Projectile from the origin,

$$S(x, y) = \sqrt{x^2 + y^2}$$

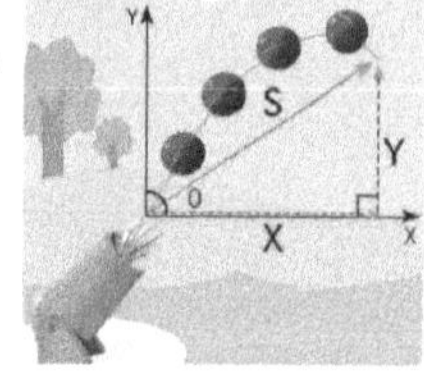

But

$$x(t) = u_0 \cos(\theta)\, t$$
$$\&$$
$$y(t) = u_0 \sin(\theta)\, t - \frac{1}{2} g\, t^2$$

Method 2: Chain rule

You know, $df=(\frac{\partial f}{\partial x})dx+(\frac{\partial f}{\partial y})dy$

$$\frac{df}{du}=(\frac{\partial f}{\partial x})\frac{dx}{du}+(\frac{\partial f}{\partial y})\frac{dy}{du}$$

Find the First differentials individually
$$\frac{\partial f}{\partial x}, \quad \frac{\partial f}{\partial y}, \quad \frac{dx}{du}, \quad \frac{dy}{du}$$
and then substitute in the above relation.

❑ Generalization for a function depends on several variables $f(x_1, x_2, x_3 \ldots x_n)$ and the variables are function of another set of variables, Let, $x_i (u_1, u_2, \ldots u_n)$

$$df= (\frac{\partial f}{\partial x_1})dx_1+ (\frac{\partial f}{\partial x_2})dx_2+\ldots\ldots+ (\frac{\partial f}{\partial x_n})dx_n= \sum_1^n (\frac{\partial f}{\partial x_i})dx_i$$

$$\frac{\partial f}{\partial u_1}= (\frac{\partial f}{\partial x_1})\frac{\partial x_1}{\partial u_1}+ (\frac{\partial f}{\partial x_2})\frac{\partial x_2}{\partial u_1}+\ldots\ldots+ (\frac{\partial f}{\partial x_n})\frac{\partial x_n}{\partial u_1} =\sum_1^n (\frac{\partial f}{\partial x_i})\frac{\partial x_i}{\partial u_1}$$

$$\frac{\partial f}{\partial u_j} = \sum_1^n (\frac{\partial f}{\partial x_i})\frac{\partial x_i}{\partial u_j}$$

In Cartesian coordinate position P is represented by (x, y).

$$\overrightarrow{OP} = \vec{r} = x\,\hat{x} + y\,\hat{y}$$

Cartesian Coordinate System

Note:

- $\hat{x}$ and $\hat{y}$ are unit vectors **pointing the increasing direction** of x and y.

- $\hat{x}$ and $\hat{y}$ are orthogonal and **points in the same direction everywhere** or for any location (x, y).

<u>Another way of looking unit vector Cartesian coordinate in plane</u>
$\hat{x}$ is the unit vector perpendicular to $x = constant$ line (surface)
$\hat{y}$ is the unit vector perpendicular to $y = constant$ line (surface)

Notations

We may interchangeably use the notations:

$$\hat{x} = \hat{\imath}$$
$$\hat{y} = \hat{\jmath}$$
$$\hat{z} = \hat{k}$$

Standard Notations:

$$\frac{dx}{dt} = \dot{x} \quad Or \quad \frac{dr}{dt} = \dot{r}$$

$$\frac{d^2\theta}{dt^2} = \ddot{\theta}$$

For **time** derivatives (only)!

Velocity $\vec{v} = \dfrac{d\vec{r}}{dt}$

Velocity in Cartesian: $\vec{v} = \dfrac{d\vec{r}}{dt} = \dfrac{d}{dt}\,(x\,\hat{x} + y\,\hat{y})$

$$= \dot{x}\hat{x} + x\,\dfrac{d\hat{x}}{dt} + \dot{y}\hat{y} + y\,\dfrac{d\hat{y}}{dt}$$

$$\boxed{\vec{v} = \dot{x}\hat{x} + \dot{y}\hat{y}}$$

Since,
$$\dfrac{d\hat{x}}{dt} = \dfrac{d\hat{y}}{dt} = 0$$

Acceleration,
$$\boxed{\vec{a} = \dfrac{d\vec{v}}{dt} = \ddot{x}\hat{x} + \ddot{y}\hat{y}}$$

Newton's second law in vector form,

$$\boxed{\vec{F} = F_x\hat{x} + F_y\hat{y} = m\,\dfrac{d\vec{v}}{dt} = m(\ddot{x}\hat{x} + \ddot{y}\hat{y})}$$

I. Plane polar coordinate

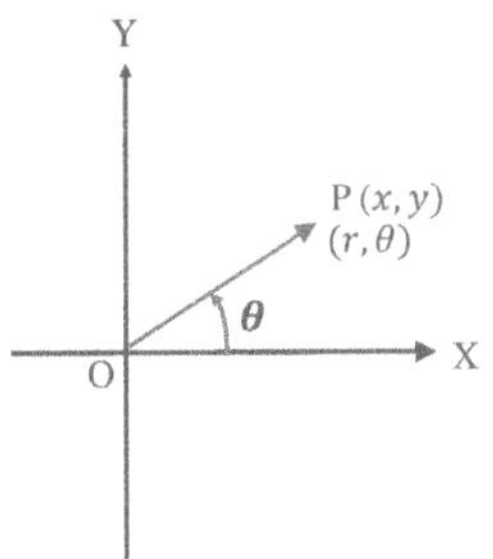

Each point P (x, y) on the plane can also be represented by its distance (r) from the origin O and the angle (θ) OP makes with X-axis.

Relationship with Cartesian coordinates

$$x = r\,\cos\theta \quad \& \quad y = r\,\sin\theta$$

Thus ,
$$r = (x^2 + y^2)^{1/2}$$
$$\theta = \tan^{-1}\dfrac{y}{x}$$

Unit vector in plane polar coordinate

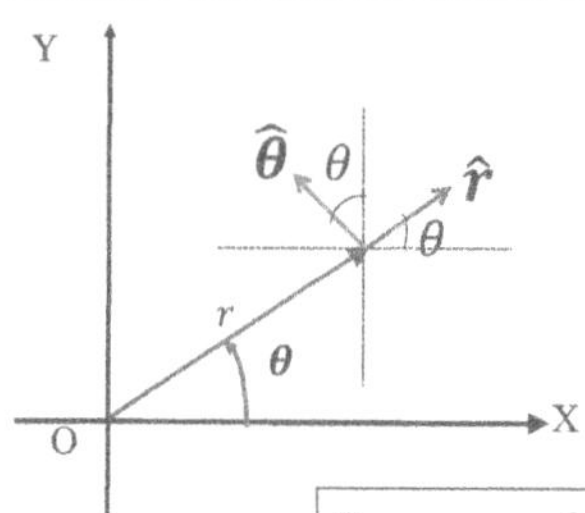

- For plane polar unit vectors:

$$\widehat{r} \text{ and } \widehat{\theta}$$

associated to **each point** in the plane.

- $\widehat{r}$ and $\widehat{\theta}$ are unit vector along increasing direction of coordinate r and θ.

$$\bar{r} = r \cos\theta \; \widehat{x} + r \sin\theta \; \widehat{y}$$

$$\widehat{r} = \cos\theta \; \widehat{x} + \sin\theta \; \widehat{y}$$
$$\widehat{\theta} = -\sin\theta \; \widehat{x} + \cos\theta \; \widehat{y}$$

$$\widehat{r} = \frac{\partial \bar{r}}{\partial r}$$

$$\widehat{\theta} = \frac{\partial \widehat{r}}{\partial \theta}$$

$\widehat{r}$ and $\widehat{\theta}$ are **orthogonal**: $\widehat{r} \cdot \widehat{\theta} = 0$ but their directions depend on location.

Unit vector in plane polar coordinate

The unit vectors in the polar coordinate can also be viewed in another way. $\widehat{r}$ is the unit vector perpendicular to $r = constant$ surface and points in the increasing direction of r.

Similarly, $\widehat{\theta}$ is the unit vector perpendicular to $\theta = constant$ surface (i,e tangential to $r = constant$) and points in the increasing direction of θ.

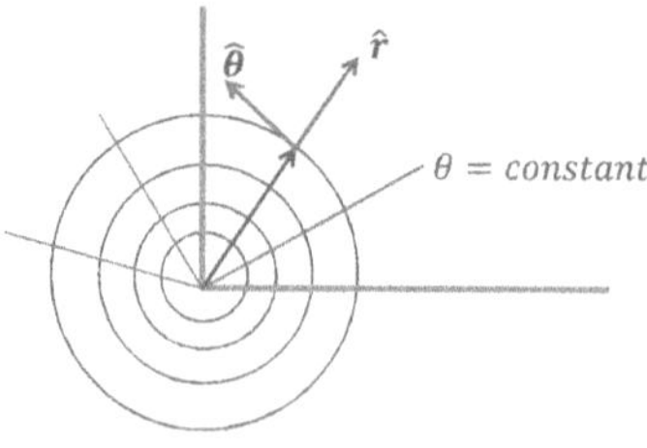

Unit vector in plane polar coordinate

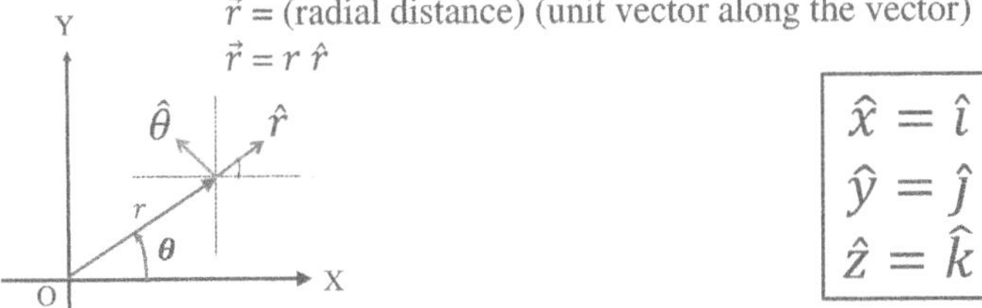

$$\vec{r} = \text{(radial distance)} \text{(unit vector along the vector)}$$
$$\vec{r} = r\,\hat{r}$$

$$\hat{x} = \hat{\imath}$$
$$\hat{y} = \hat{\jmath}$$
$$\hat{z} = \hat{k}$$

Unit vectors in polar coordinate are function of θ only.

$$\frac{\partial \hat{r}}{\partial \theta} = \frac{\partial}{\partial \theta}(\hat{x}\cos\theta + \hat{y}\sin\theta) = -\hat{x}\sin\theta + \hat{y}\cos\theta = \hat{\theta}$$

$$\frac{\partial \hat{\theta}}{\partial \theta} = \frac{\partial}{\partial \theta}(-\hat{x}\sin\theta + \hat{y}\cos\theta) = -(\hat{x}\cos\theta + \hat{y}\sin\theta) = -\hat{r}$$

Velocity in plane polar coordinate

Velocity $\vec{v} = \dfrac{d\vec{r}}{dt}$

$$\vec{v} = \frac{d\vec{r}}{dt} = \frac{d}{dt}(r\,\hat{r}) = \frac{dr}{dt}\hat{r} + r\frac{d\hat{r}}{dt}$$

$$= \dot{r}\hat{r} + r\frac{\partial \hat{r}}{\partial \theta}\frac{d\theta}{dt}$$

Since,
$$\frac{\partial \hat{r}}{\partial \theta} = \hat{\theta}$$

$$\boxed{\vec{v} = \dot{r}\hat{r} + r\dot{\theta}\hat{\theta}}$$

Radial component $\dot{r}$ and

Tangential/transverse component $r\dot{\theta}$

Acceleration in plane polar coordinate

$$\vec{a} = \frac{d\vec{v}}{dt}$$

Note: $\frac{\partial \hat{r}}{\partial \theta} = \hat{\theta}$ & $\frac{\partial \hat{\theta}}{\partial \theta} = -\hat{r}$

$$= \frac{d}{dt}(\dot{r}\hat{r} + r\dot{\theta}\hat{\theta}) \quad = \frac{d\dot{r}}{dt}\hat{r} + \dot{r}\frac{d\hat{r}}{dt} + \dot{r}\dot{\theta}\hat{\theta} + r\ddot{\theta}\hat{\theta} + r\dot{\theta}\frac{d\hat{\theta}}{dt}$$

$$= \ddot{r}\hat{r} + \dot{r}\frac{\partial \hat{r}}{\partial \theta}\frac{d\theta}{dt} + \dot{r}\dot{\theta}\hat{\theta} + r\ddot{\theta}\hat{\theta} + r\dot{\theta}\frac{\partial \hat{\theta}}{\partial \theta}\frac{d\theta}{dt}$$

$$= \ddot{r}\hat{r} + \dot{r}\dot{\theta}\hat{\theta} + \dot{r}\dot{\theta}\hat{\theta} + r\ddot{\theta}\hat{\theta} - r\dot{\theta}^2\hat{r}$$

$$\boxed{\vec{a} = (\ddot{r} - r\dot{\theta}^2)\hat{r} + (2\dot{r}\dot{\theta} + r\ddot{\theta})\hat{\theta}}$$

Radial component of acceleration: $\ddot{r} - r\dot{\theta}^2$
(Note: $-r\dot{\theta}^2$ is the familiar *Centripetal* contribution!)
Tangential component: $2\dot{r}\dot{\theta} + r\ddot{\theta}$
(Note: $2\dot{r}\dot{\theta}$ is called the *Coriolis* contribution!)

Newton's law in plane polar coordinate

$$\vec{F} = m\frac{d\vec{v}}{dt}$$

$$\vec{F} = F_r\hat{r} + F_\theta\hat{\theta} = m[(\ddot{r} - r\dot{\theta}^2)\hat{r} + (2\dot{r}\dot{\theta} + r\ddot{\theta})\hat{\theta}]$$

Newton's law for **radial** direction: $F_r = m(\ddot{r} - r\dot{\theta}^2)$

Newton's law for **tangential** direction: $F_\theta = m(2\dot{r}\dot{\theta} + r\ddot{\theta})$

Note: Newton's law in polar coordinates **do not** follow its **Cartesian form** as,

$$F_r \neq m\ddot{r} \quad \text{or} \quad F_\theta \neq m\ddot{\theta}$$

Highlights

- Transformation relation between *Cartesian* and *polar coordinate* is given by,

$$x = r \cos \theta$$
$$y = r \sin \theta$$

Reverse transformation

$$r = (x^2 + y^2)^{1/2}$$
$$\theta = \tan^{-1}\frac{y}{x}$$

- Directions of unit vectors $(\hat{x}, \hat{y})$ in **Cartesian** system remain *fixed* **irrespective** of the location (x, y).
- Directions of unit vectors $(\hat{r}, \hat{\theta})$ in **plane polar** coordinates **depend on the location**.
- **Caution:** Form of Newton's law is different in different coordinate systems.

II. Cylindrical coordinate system (r, θ, z)

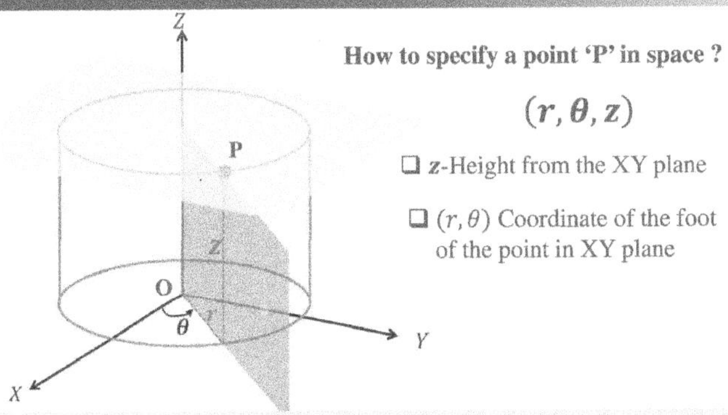

How to specify a point 'P' in space ?

$$(r, \theta, z)$$

❑ z-Height from the XY plane

❑ (r, θ) Coordinate of the foot of the point in XY plane

❑ (r, θ, z) coordinates system is known as cylindrical coordinate system

Why the name cylindrical?

❑ Point 'P' is the intersection of three surfaces: A cylindrical surface $r = constant$; A half plane containing z-axis with θ=**constant** and a plane z=**constant**.

Coordinate transformation: Cartesian to cylindrical

Transformation equation is very similar to polar coordinate with additional z-coordinate.

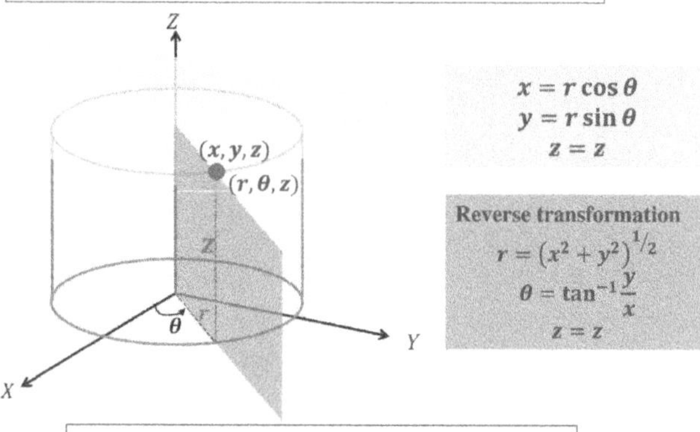

Note: Instead of (r, θ) many books use notation (ρ, φ).

Unit vectors in cylindrical coordinate system

Polar coordinate unit vectors $(\hat{r}, \hat{\theta})$ + additional unit vector in the $z-$direction.

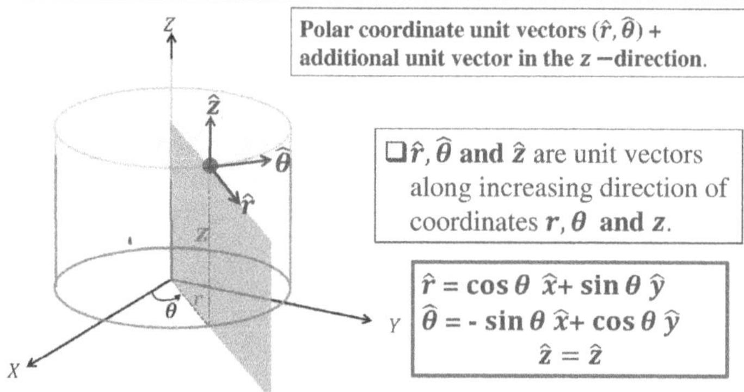

- $\hat{r}, \hat{\theta}$ and $\hat{z}$ are unit vectors along increasing direction of coordinates r, θ and z.

$$\hat{r} = \cos\theta\ \hat{x} + \sin\theta\ \hat{y}$$
$$\hat{\theta} = -\sin\theta\ \hat{x} + \cos\theta\ \hat{y}$$
$$\hat{z} = \hat{z}$$

$\hat{r}$ and $\hat{\theta}$ are **orthogonal** but their directions depend on location.

Vector components are very similar to polar coordinate+ z —component

Position vector $\Rightarrow$ $\overrightarrow{OP} = \vec{R} = r\hat{r} + z\hat{z}$

Velocity $\Rightarrow$ $\vec{v} = \dot{r}\hat{r} + r\dot{\theta}\hat{\theta} + \dot{z}\hat{z}$

Acceleration $\Rightarrow$ $\vec{a} = (\ddot{r} - r\dot{\theta}^2)\hat{r} + (2\dot{r}\dot{\theta} + r\ddot{\theta})\hat{\theta} + \ddot{z}\hat{z}$

Newton's law $\Rightarrow$
$$\vec{F} = F_r\hat{r} + F_\theta\hat{\theta} + F_z\hat{z}$$
$$= m[(\ddot{r} - r\dot{\theta}^2)\hat{r} + (2\dot{r}\dot{\theta} + r\ddot{\theta})\hat{\theta} + \ddot{z}\hat{z}]$$

III. Spherical polar coordinate system

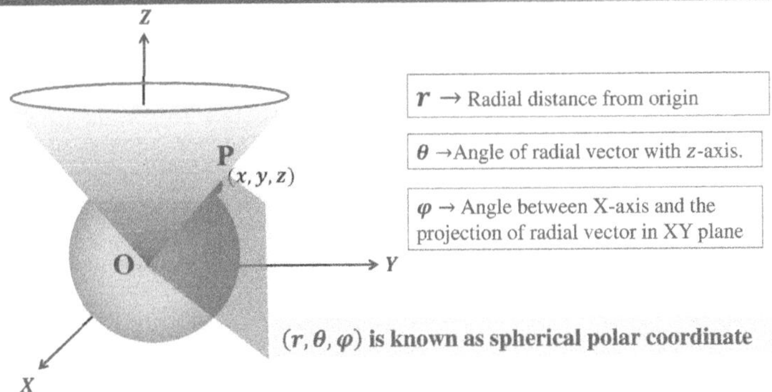

$r \rightarrow$ Radial distance from origin

$\theta \rightarrow$ Angle of radial vector with z-axis.

$\varphi \rightarrow$ Angle between X-axis and the projection of radial vector in XY plane

(r, θ, φ) is known as spherical polar coordinate

Note that point (r, θ, φ) is at the intersection of three surfaces

❑ A sphere where r =Constant

❑ A cone about z=axis with θ=constant.

❑ A half plane containing z-axis and φ= constant

Be careful, notations are different. r and θ are not planer coordinate.

Connection of spherical polar with cartesian

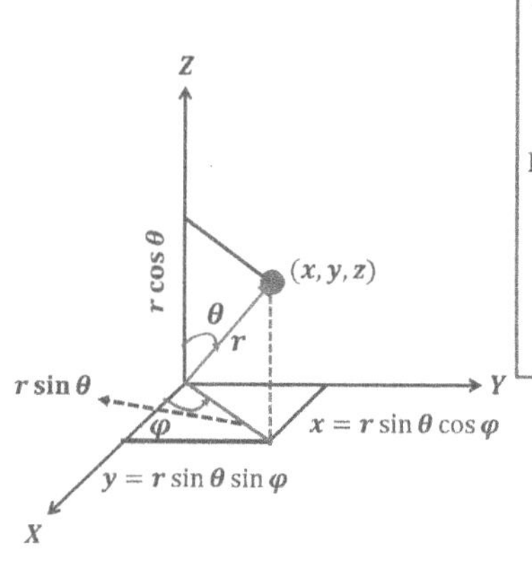

Transformation relations
$$x = r \sin\theta \cos\varphi$$
$$y = r \sin\theta \sin\varphi$$
$$z = r \cos\theta$$

Hence
$$r = \left(x^2 + y^2 + z^2\right)^{1/2}$$
$$\theta = \tan^{-1}\frac{\left(x^2 + y^2\right)^{1/2}}{z}$$
$$\varphi = \tan^{-1}\frac{y}{x}$$

Unit vectors in spherical polar

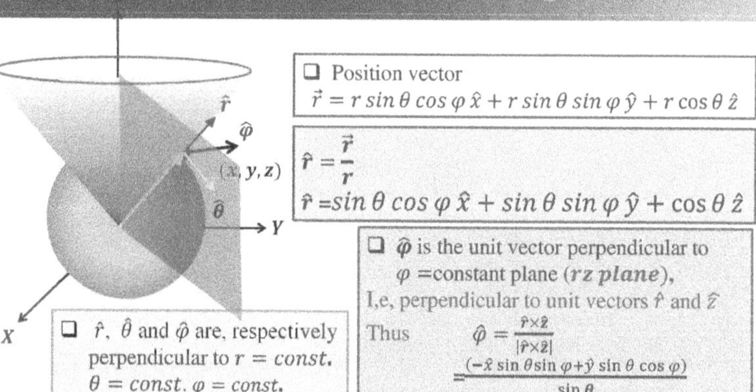

❑ Position vector
$$\vec{r} = r \sin\theta \cos\varphi\, \hat{x} + r \sin\theta \sin\varphi\, \hat{y} + r \cos\theta\, \hat{z}$$

$$\hat{r} = \frac{\vec{r}}{r}$$
$$\hat{r} = \sin\theta \cos\varphi\, \hat{x} + \sin\theta \sin\varphi\, \hat{y} + \cos\theta\, \hat{z}$$

❑ $\hat{\varphi}$ is the unit vector perpendicular to
$\varphi =$ constant plane ($rz\ plane$),
I,e, perpendicular to unit vectors $\hat{r}$ and $\hat{z}$

Thus
$$\hat{\varphi} = \frac{\hat{r}\times\hat{z}}{|\hat{r}\times\hat{z}|}$$
$$= \frac{(-\hat{x}\sin\theta\sin\varphi + \hat{y}\sin\theta\cos\varphi)}{\sin\theta}$$
$$\hat{\varphi} = -\hat{x}\sin\varphi + \hat{y}\cos\varphi$$

❑ $\hat{r}$, $\hat{\theta}$ and $\hat{\varphi}$ are, respectively
perpendicular to $r = const.$
$\theta = const.$ $\varphi = const.$

❑ $\hat{\theta} = \dfrac{(\hat{\varphi}\times\hat{r})}{|\hat{\varphi}\times\hat{r}|}$
$$= \hat{x}\cos\varphi\cos\theta + \hat{y}\sin\varphi\cos\theta - \hat{z}\sin\theta$$

Unit vectors in spherical polar

$$\vec{r} = r\sin\theta\cos\varphi\,\hat{x} + r\sin\theta\sin\varphi\,\hat{y} + r\cos\theta\,\hat{z}$$

$$\hat{r} = \frac{\vec{r}}{r} = \hat{x}\cos\varphi\sin\theta + \hat{y}\sin\varphi\sin\theta + \hat{z}\cos\theta$$

$$\hat{\theta} = \frac{\partial\hat{r}}{\partial\theta} = \hat{x}\cos\varphi\cos\theta + \hat{y}\sin\varphi\cos\theta - \hat{z}\sin\theta$$

$$\hat{\varphi} = -\hat{x}\sin\varphi + \hat{y}\cos\varphi \;\; (\equiv \hat{\theta}\ of\ Plane\ Polar\ \theta \to \varphi!)$$

Partial differential of unit vectors in spherical polar

Unit vectors in spherical polar coordinate are function of θ and φ only.

$$\frac{\partial\hat{r}}{\partial\theta} = \frac{\partial}{\partial\theta}(\hat{x}\sin\theta\cos\varphi + \hat{y}\sin\theta\sin\varphi + \hat{z}\cos\theta)$$
$$= (\hat{x}\cos\theta\cos\varphi + \hat{y}\cos\theta\sin\varphi - \hat{z}\sin\theta) = \hat{\theta}$$

$$\frac{\partial\hat{r}}{\partial\varphi} = \frac{\partial}{\partial\varphi}(\hat{x}\sin\theta\cos\varphi + \hat{y}\sin\theta\sin\varphi + \hat{z}\cos\theta)$$
$$= (-\hat{x}\sin\theta\sin\varphi + \hat{y}\sin\theta\cos\varphi) = \sin\theta\,\hat{\varphi}$$

Additionally, you may verify:

$$\frac{\partial\hat{\theta}}{\partial\theta} = \frac{\partial}{\partial\theta}(\hat{x}\cos\theta\cos\varphi + \hat{y}\cos\theta\sin\varphi - \hat{z}\sin\theta)$$
$$= (-\hat{x}\sin\theta\cos\varphi - \hat{y}\sin\theta\cos\varphi - \hat{z}\cos\theta) = -\hat{r}$$

$$\frac{\partial\hat{\theta}}{\partial\varphi} = \frac{\partial}{\partial\varphi}(\hat{x}\cos\theta\cos\varphi + \hat{y}\cos\theta\sin\varphi - \hat{z}\sin\theta)$$
$$= (-\hat{x}\cos\theta\sin\varphi + \hat{y}\cos\theta\cos\varphi) = -\cos\theta\,\hat{r}$$

Velocity in spherical polar coordinate

$$\vec{r} = r\sin\theta\cos\varphi\,\hat{x} + r\sin\theta\sin\varphi\,\hat{y} + r\cos\theta\,\hat{z}$$

$$\vec{v} = \frac{d\vec{r}}{dt} = \frac{d}{dt}(r\hat{r})$$

$$= \frac{dr}{dt}\hat{r} + r\frac{d\hat{r}}{dt}$$

$$= \dot{r}\hat{r} + r\left(\frac{\partial\hat{r}}{\partial\theta}\frac{d\theta}{dt} + \frac{\partial\hat{r}}{\partial\varphi}\frac{d\varphi}{dt}\right) \quad \longleftarrow \quad \boxed{\text{Chain rule}}$$

$$= \dot{r}\hat{r} + r\left(\dot{\theta}\hat{\theta} + \sin\theta\,\dot{\varphi}\,\hat{\varphi}\right)$$

$$\boxed{\vec{v} = \dot{r}\hat{r} + r\dot{\theta}\hat{\theta} + r\sin\theta\,\dot{\varphi}\,\hat{\varphi}}$$

Acceleration — You must try to prove this

$$\vec{a}$$
$$= \left(\ddot{r} - r\dot{\theta}^2 - r\dot{\varphi}^2\sin^2\theta\right)\hat{r} + \left(r\ddot{\theta} - 2\dot{r}\dot{\theta} - r\dot{\varphi}^2\sin\theta\cos\theta\right)\hat{\theta} + \left(r\ddot{\varphi}\sin\theta + 2r\dot{\theta}\dot{\varphi}\cos\theta + 2\dot{r}\dot{\varphi}\sin\theta\right)\hat{\varphi}$$

Velocity –to remember!

Elementary displacement in arbitrary direction $\overrightarrow{\Delta r}$ in Δt

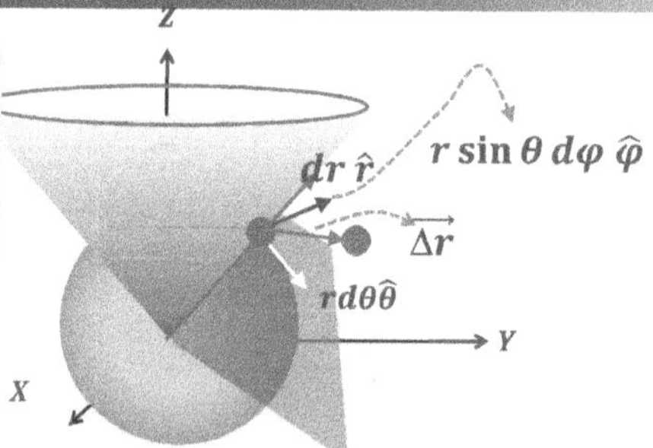

$$\overrightarrow{\Delta r} = dr\,\hat{r} + rd\theta\,\hat{\theta} + r\sin\theta\,d\varphi\,\hat{\varphi}$$

$$\vec{v} = \frac{\overrightarrow{\Delta r}}{\Delta t} = \frac{dr}{\Delta t}\hat{r} + \frac{rd\theta}{\Delta t}\hat{\theta} + \frac{r\sin\theta\,d\varphi}{\Delta t}\hat{\varphi}$$

$$\vec{v} = \dot{r}\hat{r} + r\dot{\theta}\hat{\theta} + r\sin\theta\,\dot{\varphi}\,\hat{\varphi}$$

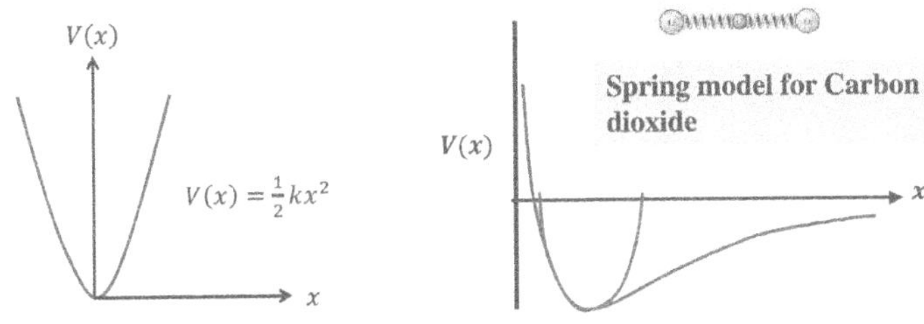

Harmonic approximation of potential energy

$V(x)$

$V(x) = \frac{1}{2}kx^2$

x

Spring model for Carbon dioxide

$V(x)$

x

| Pure harmonic potential | Harmonic approximation of the potential |

❑ Potential energy for atom and many other practical systems are close to harmonic around equilibrium point but deviates at larger distance from equilibrium

❑ Exact potential is hard to solve.

Harmonic approximation

Taylor series/expansion

$$V(x) = V(x_0) + V'(x_0)(x - x_0) + \frac{1}{2!}V''(x_0)(x - x_0)^2 + O(3)$$

Here $V'(x) = \frac{dV}{dx}$ and $V''(x) = \frac{d^2V}{dx^2}$

❑ Here we are taking the expansion around the equilibrium distance x_0.

Hence $V'(x_0) = 0$ since the force is zero (potential has an extremum).

❑ Let us assume that $V(x_0) = 0$, the potential at the equilibrium (reference) is zero.

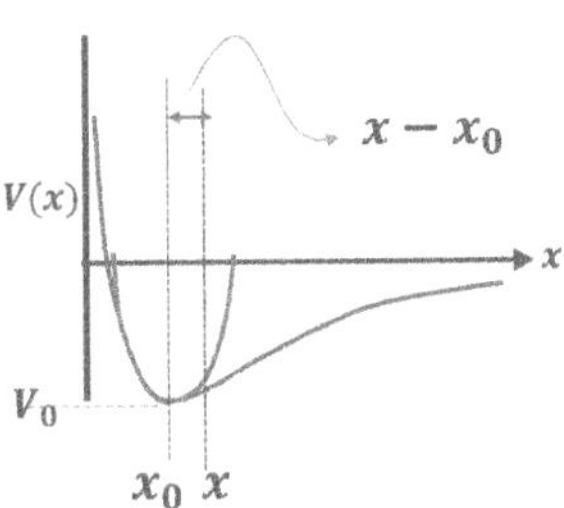

$$e^x = 1 + x + \frac{x^2}{2!} + \frac{x^3}{3!} + \frac{x^4}{4!} + \ldots$$

$$\sin x = x - \frac{x^3}{3!} + \frac{x^5}{5!} - \frac{x^7}{7!} + \ldots$$

$$\cos x = 1 - \frac{x^2}{2!} + \frac{x^4}{4!} - \frac{x^6}{6!} + \ldots$$

$$\ln(1 + x) = x - \frac{x^2}{2} + \frac{x^3}{3} - \frac{x^4}{4} + \ldots \quad for\,|x| < 1$$

Harmonic approximation continue..

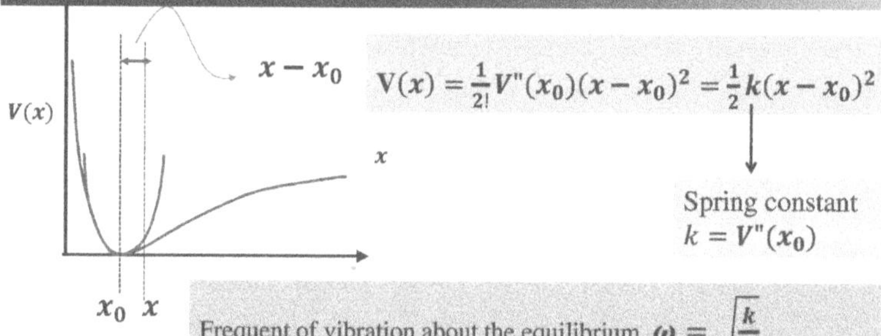

$$V(x) = \frac{1}{2!}V''(x_0)(x - x_0)^2 = \frac{1}{2}k(x - x_0)^2$$

Spring constant
$k = V''(x_0)$

Frequent of vibration about the equilibrium, $\omega = \sqrt{\dfrac{k}{m}}$,

For two particle system (molecule),

$$\text{frequency of vibration } \omega = \sqrt{\frac{k}{\mu}}$$

Where, $Reduced\ mass(\mu)\ of\ oscillitator$

$$\mu = \frac{m_1 m_2}{m_1 + m_2}$$

Harmonic approximation: Example

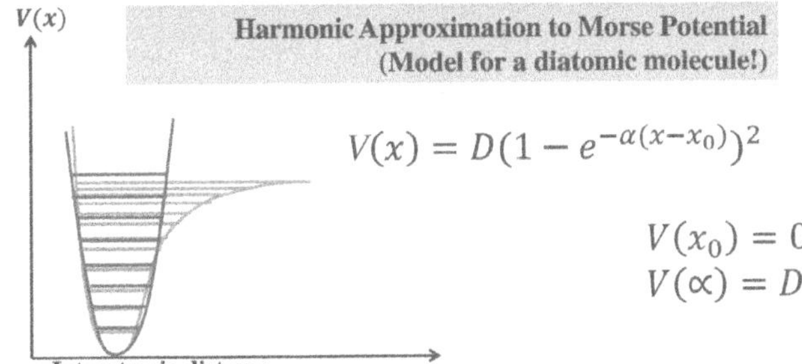

$$V(x) = D\left(1 - e^{-\alpha(x-x_0)}\right)^2$$

$$V(x_0) = 0$$
$$V(\infty) = D$$

To break the molecule one has to supply energy D. This is a convenient model for diatomic molecules.

Harmonic approximation: Morse Potential

First find the equilibrium

$$V'(x) = 2D\alpha\left(1 - e^{-\alpha(x-x_0)}\right)\, e^{-\alpha(x-x_0)} = 0$$

Solving, at equilibrium $x = x_0$

Now $V''(x) = 2D\alpha\left(-\alpha e^{-\alpha(x-x_0)} + 2\alpha e^{-2\alpha(x-x_0)}\right)$

At equilibrium $V''(x_0) = 2D\alpha^2 \approx k$

$$\omega = \sqrt{\frac{k}{\mu}} = \alpha\sqrt{2D/\mu}$$

Work and potential energy in 3D

1D motion: Displacement and force are along the same line

Work done by force
$$dW = F\,dx = -dV$$
Thus, $F = -\dfrac{dV}{dx}$

3D motion: Displacement and force are in different directions
$$dW = F\cos\theta\,dr$$
$$dW = \vec{F}\cdot d\vec{r} = F_x dx + F_y dy + F_z dz$$
$$= -dV$$
$$\vec{F} =?$$

$\vec{F} = F_x\hat{x} + F_y\hat{y} + F_z\hat{z}$

$d\vec{r} = dx\,\hat{x} + dy\,\hat{y} + dz\,\hat{z}$

$$dV = -\vec{F}\cdot d\vec{r} = -(F_x dx + F_y dy + F_z dz)$$

dV in 2D and 3D?

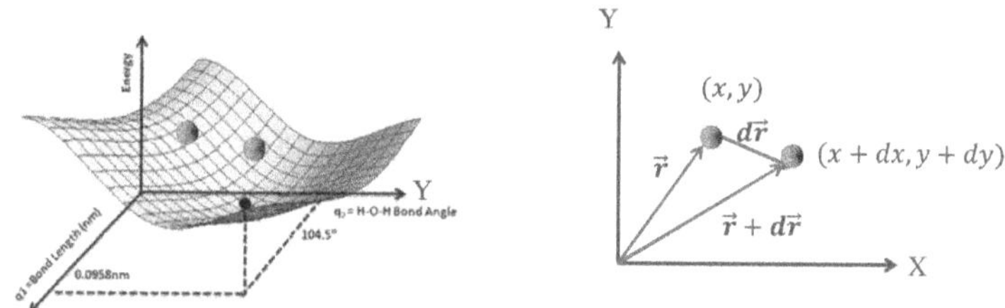

Rate of change of potential energy is different in different directions

Total change in potential energy due to change of x by dx and y by dy
$$dV = \frac{\partial V}{\partial x}dx + \frac{\partial V}{\partial y}dy$$

3D: Since, $V(x, y, z)$

$$dV = \frac{\partial V}{\partial x}dx + \frac{\partial V}{\partial y}dy + \frac{\partial V}{\partial z}dz$$

Potential energy in 3D

We can write

$$dV = \frac{\partial V}{\partial x}dx + \frac{\partial V}{\partial y}dy + \frac{\partial V}{\partial z}dz$$

$$= \left(\frac{\partial V}{\partial x}\hat{x} + \frac{\partial V}{\partial y}\hat{y} + \frac{\partial V}{\partial z}\hat{z}\right) \cdot (\hat{x}dx + \hat{y}dy + \hat{z}dz)$$

$$dV = \left(\frac{\partial}{\partial x}\hat{x} + \frac{\partial}{\partial y}\hat{y} + \frac{\partial}{\partial z}\hat{z}\right)V \cdot (\hat{x}dx + \hat{y}dy + \hat{z}dz)$$

$$\boldsymbol{dV = \vec{\nabla}V \cdot d\vec{r}}$$

$\vec{\nabla}$ symbols stands for an operator $\quad \vec{\nabla} = \frac{\partial}{\partial x}\hat{x} + \frac{\partial}{\partial y}\hat{y} + \frac{\partial}{\partial z}\hat{z}$

$\vec{\nabla}V$ -this operation is know as **gradient of V**

Since, $\qquad dV = -\vec{F} \cdot d\vec{r}$

$$\boldsymbol{\vec{F} = -\vec{\nabla}V}$$

$$F_x = -\frac{\partial V}{\partial x} \qquad\qquad F_y = -\frac{\partial V}{\partial y} \qquad\qquad F_z = -\frac{\partial V}{\partial z}$$

Gradient in plane polar!

Let we have, $V(r, \theta)$

$$dV = \frac{\partial V}{\partial r}dr + \frac{\partial V}{\partial \theta}d\theta \qquad \text{(by rule!)}$$

But, $\quad dV = -\vec{F} \cdot d\vec{r} = -\left(F_r\hat{r} + F_\theta\hat{\theta}\right) \cdot \left(dr\,\hat{r} + rd\theta\,\widehat{\theta}\right)$

$$= -(F_r dr + F_\theta r d\theta)$$

$$F_r = -\frac{\partial V}{\partial r} \qquad \& \qquad F_\theta = -\frac{1}{r}\frac{\partial V}{\partial \theta}$$

Or, $\quad dV = \vec{\nabla}V \cdot d\vec{r} = -\left(F_r\hat{r} + F_\theta\hat{\theta}\right)$

$$\Rightarrow \qquad \vec{\nabla} = \frac{\partial(\ )}{\partial r}\hat{r} + \frac{1}{r}\frac{\partial(\ )}{\partial \theta}\widehat{\theta} \qquad \text{(in plane polar)}$$

Note: Conservative vs non-conservative forces

$$\vec{F} = -\vec{\nabla}V \quad \text{(true only for conservative forces ?)}$$

Let's review how we have arrived to this relation:
We have assumed that
Work done by the force is entirely stored in the system as potential energy,
$$-dW = dV$$

Work done by all type of forces do not converted to potential energy stored in the system, it may lost by dissipation in the form of heat, sound etc. Those forces are dissipative force/non-conservative force, **Example: Friction**

Work done by dissipative force $dW = \vec{f} \cdot d\vec{r} \neq dV$,
Energy is not stored as potential energy.
Hence $\vec{f} \neq -\vec{\nabla}V$
$T + V \neq constant$ when a particle is under dissipative forces. Thus they are non-conservative force.

Note: Conservative force

Is the force always derivable from scalar potential $\vec{F} = -\vec{\nabla}V$?
Answer is no, all forces are not derivable from scalar potential.

Those forces which are derivable from scalar potential ($\vec{F} = -\vec{\nabla}V$) are known as **conservative force**.

Work done due to motion from A to B

$$dW = \vec{F} \cdot d\vec{r} = -\vec{\nabla}V \cdot d\vec{r} = -dV \; ; thus \; W = -\int_{A}^{B} dV = V_A - V_B$$

$$Agian, dW = \vec{F} \cdot d\vec{r} = m\frac{d\vec{v}}{dt} \cdot d\vec{r} = m\frac{d\vec{v}}{dt} \cdot \vec{v}dt = \frac{1}{2}md(\vec{v} \cdot \vec{v}) = \frac{1}{2}m\,d(v^2)$$

$$W = \int_{A}^{B} \frac{1}{2}m\,d(v^2) = \frac{1}{2}mv_B^2 - \frac{1}{2}mv_A^2 \; (= Change \; in \; K.E.)$$

$$Thus, \; V_A - V_B = \frac{1}{2}mv_B^2 - \frac{1}{2}mv_A^2 \Rightarrow V_A + \frac{1}{2}mv_A^2 = V_B + \frac{1}{2}mv_B^2$$

Energy conserved (True for conservative force)

Conservative forces

For a conservative force $\vec{F} = -\vec{\nabla}V$, where $\vec{\nabla} = \frac{\partial}{\partial x}\hat{x} + \frac{\partial}{\partial y}\hat{y} + \frac{\partial}{\partial z}\hat{z}$

For a conservative force what will be the value of $\vec{\nabla} \times \vec{F}$?

Let's remember that: $\vec{A} \times \vec{B} = \begin{vmatrix} \hat{x} & \hat{y} & \hat{z} \\ A_x & A_y & A_z \\ B_x & B_y & F_z \end{vmatrix}$

❏ **"Curl"** of a vector in Cartesian

$$\vec{\nabla} \times \vec{F} = \begin{vmatrix} \hat{x} & \hat{y} & \hat{z} \\ \frac{\partial}{\partial x} & \frac{\partial}{\partial y} & \frac{\partial}{\partial z} \\ F_x & F_y & F_z \end{vmatrix} = \hat{x}\left(\frac{\partial F_z}{\partial y} - \frac{\partial F_y}{\partial z}\right) + \hat{y}\left(\frac{\partial F_x}{\partial z} - \frac{\partial F_z}{\partial x}\right) + \hat{z}\left(\frac{\partial F_y}{\partial x} - \frac{\partial F_x}{\partial y}\right)$$

$$\frac{\partial F_z}{\partial y} = \frac{\partial(-\frac{\partial V}{\partial z})}{\partial y} = -\frac{\partial^2 V}{\partial y \partial z} \quad \& \quad \frac{\partial F_y}{\partial z} = \frac{\partial(\frac{-\partial V}{\partial y})}{\partial z} = -\frac{\partial^2 V}{\partial z \partial y}$$

But, $\frac{\partial^2 V}{\partial x \partial y} = \frac{\partial^2 V}{\partial y \partial x}$

(order is immeterial by rule!)

For a conservative force: $\qquad \vec{\nabla} \times \vec{F} = 0$

Summmery

❏ **Taylor series expansion of a potential in 1D**

$$V(x) = V(x_0) + V'(x_0)(x - x_0) + \frac{1}{2!}V''(x_0)(x - x_0)^2 + O(3)$$

Here $V'(x) = \frac{dU}{dx}$ and $V''(x) = \frac{d^2V}{dx^2}$

Harmonic approximation consider only upto square term

Frequency of oscillation $\omega = \sqrt{\frac{k}{\mu}}$, $\quad k = U''(x_0)$, and μ is the reduced mass.

So, if

$$\vec{F} = -\vec{\nabla}V \qquad \text{(“gradient” of V)}$$

"Curl" of F, $\qquad \vec{\nabla} \times \vec{F} = 0 \qquad$ (always!)

Curl of gradient is always zero $\left(\vec{\nabla} \times \vec{\nabla}f = 0\right)$ (for any scalar function)

Constrains

Motion of particle not always remains free but often is subjected to given conditions.

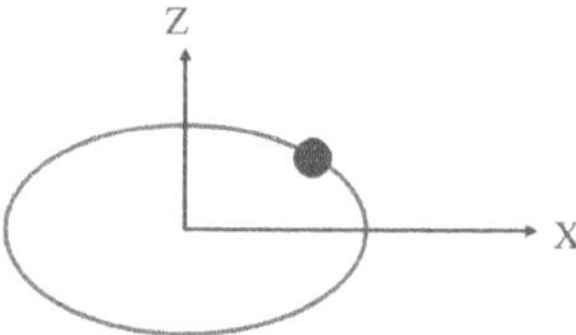

A particle is bound to move along the circumference of an ellipse in XZ plane.

At all position of the particle, it is bound to obey the condition $\frac{x^2}{a^2} + \frac{z^2}{b^2} = 1$

Constrains: Condition or restrictions imposed on motion of particle/particles

Classification of constrains

❑ **Holonomic Constrains:** Expressible in terms of equation involving coordinates and time (may or may not present),

I,e. $f(q_1, \ldots q_n, t) = 0$;   where q_i are the instantaneous coordinates

❑ **Non-holonomic constrains :** Constrains which are not holonomic

Two types of constrains are there in this category

(i) *Equations involving velocities*: $f(q_1, \ldots, \dot{q}_1, \ldots, \dot{q}_n, t) = 0$,
(& those cannot be **reduced** to the holonomic form!).

(ii) Constraints as *in-equalities*,
An example, $f(q_1, \ldots, q_n, t) < 0$

In both type of constrains (holonomic/non-holonomic) time may or may not be present explicitly.

Pendulum

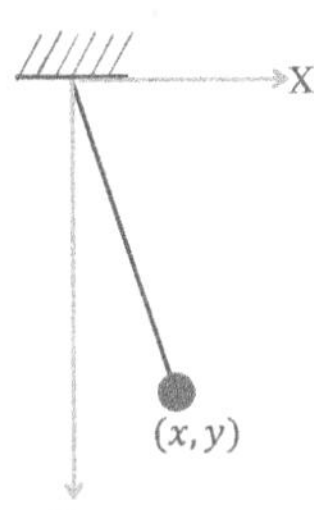

□ *Constrain equations*
$$x^2 + y^2 = l^2$$
$$x = \sqrt{l^2 - y^2}$$

□ One can not change x **independently**, any change in x will automatically change y.

x, y *are not independent* **due to presence of constrains**

Independent coordinates: If you fix all but one coordinate and still have a continuous range of movement in the free coordinate.

If you fix y_1, leaving x_1 free, then there is no continuous range of x_1 possible. In fact in this case there will not be any motion if you fix y_1

Degree of Freedom &Generalized coordinate

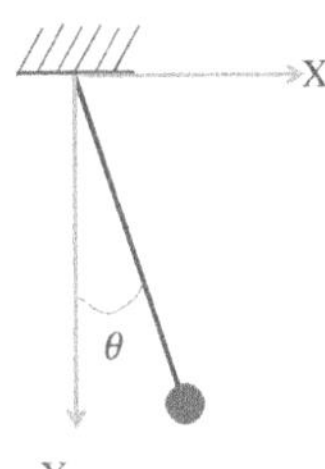

□ If you choose θ as the only coordinate, it can represent entire motion of the bob in XY plane

□ In this problem, only one coordinate θ is sufficient which is sole independent coordinate.

Degree of Freedom (DOF): no of independent coordinate required to represent the entire motion = $3 \times$ (*no of particles*) $-$ *no. of constrains* $=3-2=1$

In this case no. of particle=1
No. of constrains =2   [$x^2 + y^2 = l^2$ and $z = 0$]

DOF =1; Generalized Coordinate= θ

Degree's of freedom

- **Degree's of freedom (DOF):** No. of independent coordinates required to completely specify the dynamics of particles/system of particles is known as degree's of freedom.

- Degree's of freedom =
  $3 \times (no.\,of\,particles) - (No.\,of\,holonomic\,constrains)$

$$= 3N - k$$

Where
N = No. of particles
k = No. of constrains.

Holonomic constrains

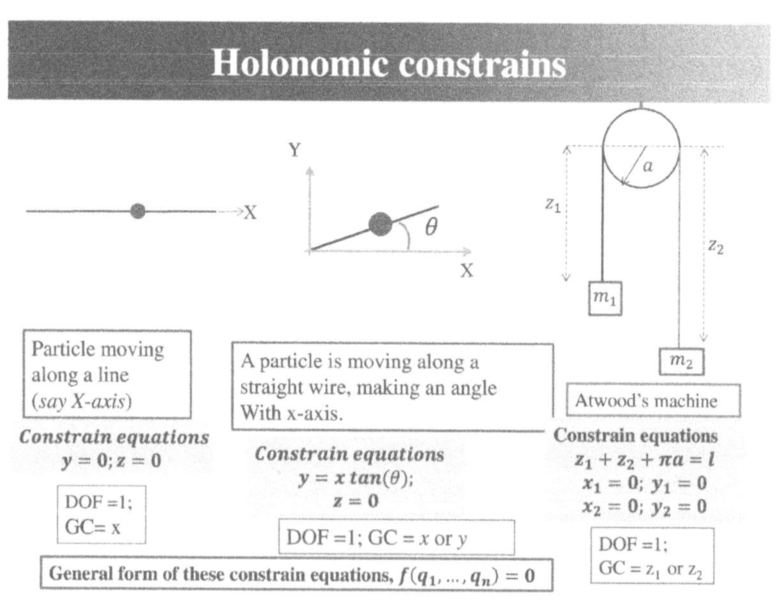

Particle moving along a line (*say X-axis*)	A particle is moving along a straight wire, making an angle With x-axis.	Atwood's machine
Constrain equations $y = 0; z = 0$	*Constrain equations* $y = x\,tan(\theta);$ $z = 0$	*Constrain equations* $z_1 + z_2 + \pi a = l$ $x_1 = 0; y_1 = 0$ $x_2 = 0; y_2 = 0$
DOF =1; GC= x	DOF =1; GC = x or y	DOF =1; GC = z_1 or z_2

General form of these constrain equations, $f(q_1, \dots, q_n) = 0$

Pendulum of varying length!

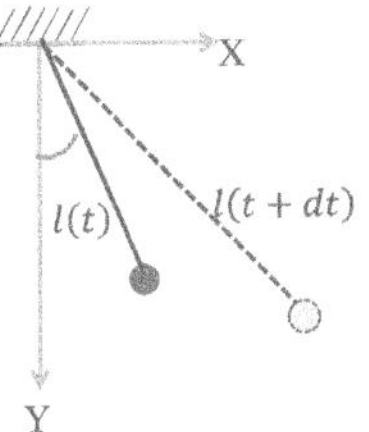

The length of the string is changing with time $l(t)$ and **is known.**

General form of these constrain equations $f(q_1, \ldots, q_n, t) = 0$

Pendulum with stretchable string, the bob is constrain to move in a plane

Constrain equations
$$x^2 + y^2 = l^2(t)$$
$$z = 0$$

DOF = 1; GC = θ

Non-holonomic constraint

Gas molecules confined within a spherical container of radius R

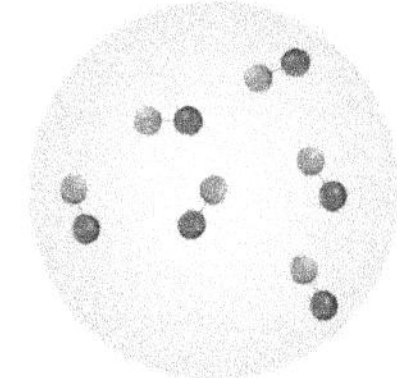

Constrain condition $r_i \leq R$

Inequality!

Rolling Constraint

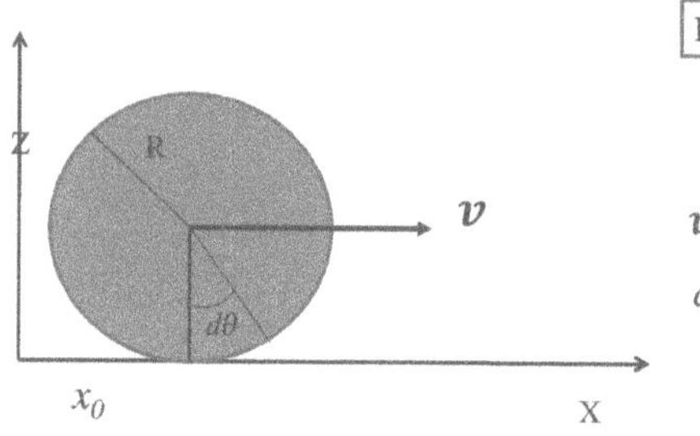

Rolling of a disc without slipping

$$v = R\dot{\theta}$$

$$dx = Rd\theta$$

$$x - R\theta = x_0 \quad \text{(constraint relation)}$$

DOF $=1$; GC $= \theta$

Other *Constrains*:
$y = 0; z = R; \varphi = 0; \psi = 0;$

More complicated constraint

Speed,
$$v = R\dot{\varphi}$$

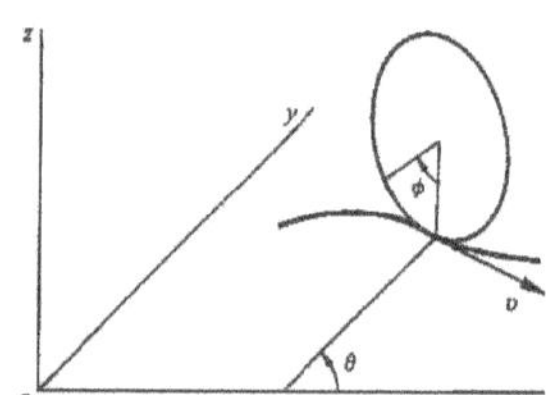

$$\dot{x} = v \sin\theta = R\dot{\varphi}\sin\theta$$

$$\dot{y} = -v \cos\theta = -R\dot{\varphi}\cos\theta$$

Velocity dependence that can't be integrated out!
Non-holonomic!

Double pendulum

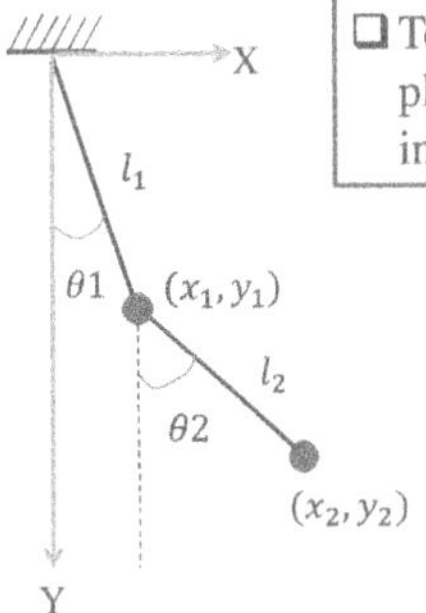

❑ To describe the motion double pendulum in XY plane, one needs four coordinates (x_1, y_1, x_2, y_2) in Cartesian coordinate system.

❑ The Cartesian coordinates are **not independent**, they are related by constrain equations

$$x_1^2 + y_1^2 = l_1^2$$
$$(x_2 - x_1)^2 + (y_2 - y_1)^2 = l_2^2$$

If you fix y_1, x_2, y_2 leaving x_1 free, then there is no continuous range of x_1 possible. In fact in this case there will not be any motion by fixing three coordinates leaving one as free.

Generalizer coordinates

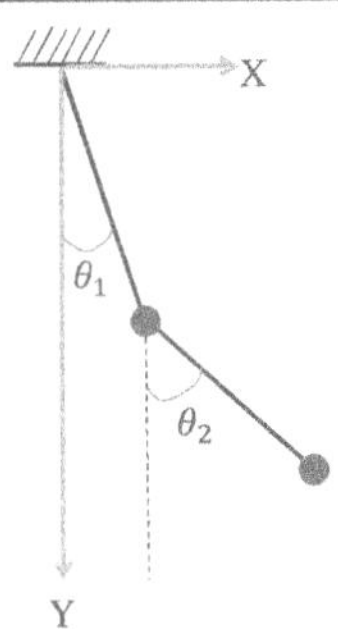

❑ If you choose θ_1 and θ_2 as the coordinates, then they can adequately describe the motion of double pendulum at any instant. (they are complete)

No. of constrains = 4
$z_1 = 0; z_2 = 0;$
$x_1^2 + y_1^2 = l_1^2;$
$(x_2 - x_1)^2 + (y_2 - y_1)^2 = l_2^2$

DOF: No. of independent coordinates required to completely specify the motion
$= 3 \times (no.\ of\ particles) - (No.\ of\ constrains)$
$= 3 \times 2 - 4 = 2$

Generalizer coordinates: θ_1 and θ_2

Generalized coordinate?

❑ **Generalized coordinate**
➢ non necessarily a distance
➢ Not necessarily an angle.
➢ **Not necessarily belong to a particular coordinate system!**
(Cartesian, Cylindrical, Polar or Spherical polar)

> **Let's check an example to clarify the above mentioned points**

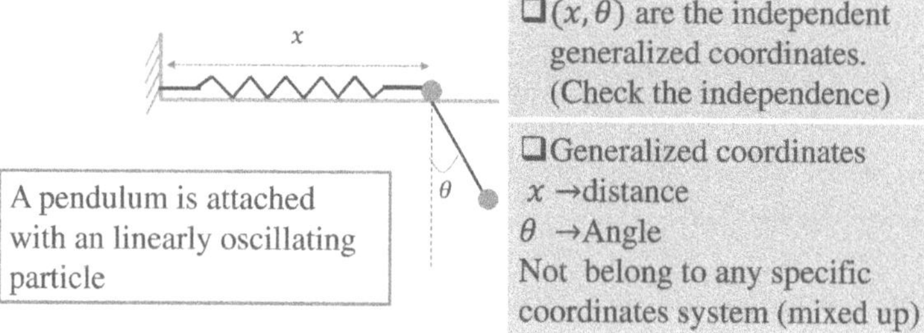

A pendulum is attached with an linearly oscillating particle

❑ (x, θ) are the independent generalized coordinates. (Check the independence)

❑ Generalized coordinates
$x \rightarrow$ distance
$\theta \rightarrow$ Angle
Not belong to any specific coordinates system (mixed up)

Generalized coordinates properties

❑ $q_j \rightarrow$ **To be generalized coordinates**
They must be
➢ Must be independent
➢ Must be complete
➢ System must be holonomic

❑ **Meaning of Complete**: Capable to describe the system configuration at times. In other word, capable of locating all parts at all times.

❑ Generalized coordinates
➢ Not necessarily Cartesian
➢ Not necessarily any specific coordinate system

Generalized coordinates of rigid body

❑ **Rigid body has six degrees of freedom**
Thus **six generalized coordinates** are necessary to specify the
dynamics of rigid body

**3 translational DOF for the center of Mass + 3 rotational degree
of freedom about the center of mass = 6 generalized coordinates**

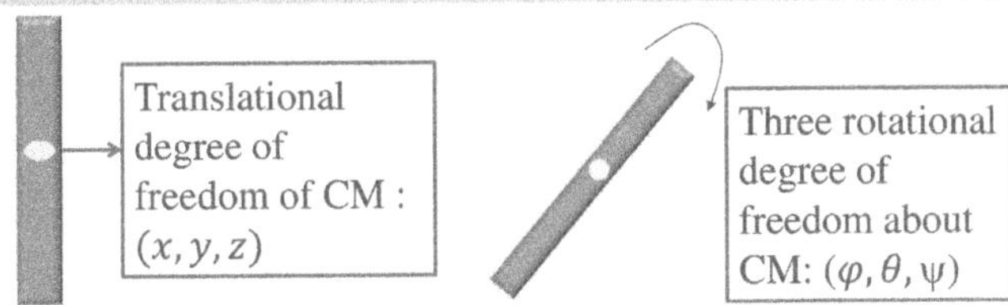

In case of only translation (motion of CM), a rigid body
can be accounted as point particle during estimating the
number degree of freedom

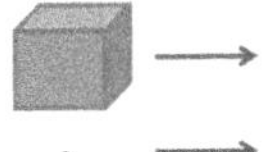

Summery

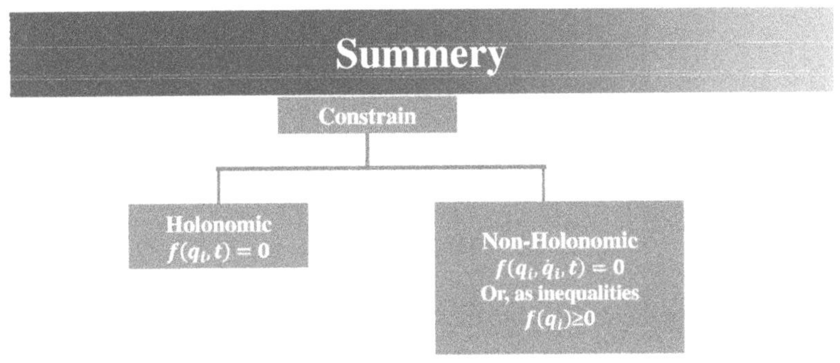

❑ Degree's of freedom =No. of **independent** coordinates required to completely specify
particles configuration at all times (generalized coordinates) $= 3N - k$
Where N→ no. of particles
$k \rightarrow$ no. of holonomic, constrains

❑ Choice of generalized coordinates is not unique but no. must be equal to degree's of
freedom.

The difficulty with Newton's Scheme

Newton's 2nd Law:
$$\vec{F} = m\frac{d^2\ddot{\vec{r}}}{dt^2}$$

$$m\frac{d^2\ddot{\vec{r}}}{dt^2} = \vec{F}_e + \vec{f}_c \qquad \text{where, } \vec{F} = \vec{F}_e + \vec{f}_c$$

$\vec{F}_e = \boldsymbol{vector}$ sum of the external forces (***known***)

$\vec{f}_c = \boldsymbol{vector}$ sum of the Constraint forces (***unknown***)

To solve the equation(s), we need to know all the **constrain force(s) $\vec{f}_c$**

General difficulty with Newton's Scheme:

- Constrain equations $f(x, t) = 0$ is known for a problem but constraint force(s) is still unknown. Finding the constraint forces are not always very obvious.

- Handling too many constrain forces and their components for a system of particles is very cumbersome.

Constraints Forces…the difficulty with Newton's Scheme

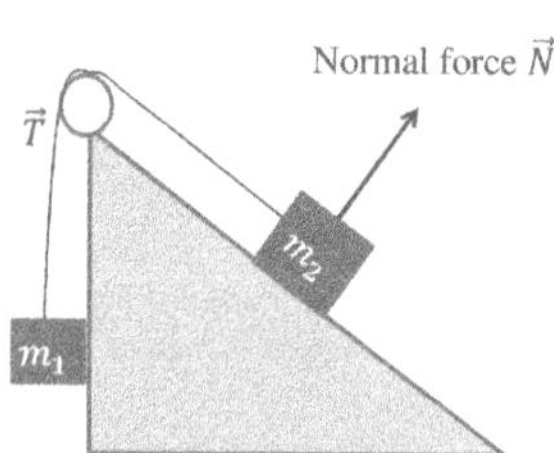

Two masses are connected by string of length l. Mass m_2 slides down the inclined frictionless plane.
Different sort of constraint forces involved

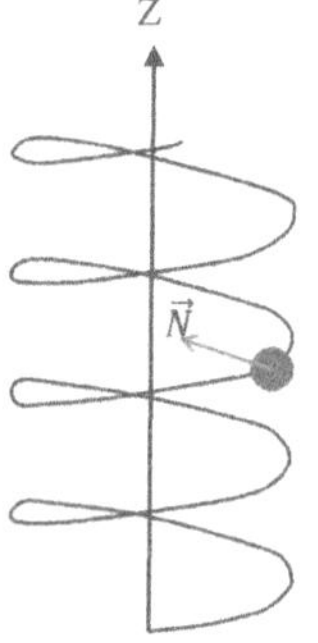

A particle is sliding down a spiral: *Direction of constraint forces changing continuously*

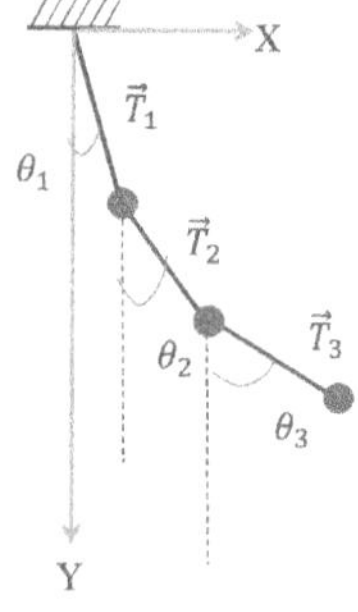

Too many constraint forces and their components to deal with

Our life would be easier if
(1) There exists a **new recipe, an alternative to Newton's Scheme,**
which **does not require** to consider **constraint forces,**
    instead **utilize** the **constraint relations.**

(2) Further, it will be ideal if the new recipe does not depend on any specific
coordinate system. Then we may be able to utilize the symmetry of the
problem, which would simplify the dynamical equations.

Good News

There is one alternative formalism to Newtonian scheme which **does not
require** to consider **constraint forces** and also **independent** of the choice of the
coordinate system:

The **Euler-Largrange** equations!

Joseph-Louis Lagrange

Born, 1736, Turin, Italy. – Died, 1813, Paris, France.

Known for his contributions to:
        Analytical mechanics
        Calculus of Variations
        Astronomy

Introduce a new function:

$$\textbf{\textit{Lagrangian:}} \quad L(q_1, \dots, q_n, \dot{q}_1, \dots, \dot{q}_n, t)$$

Defined as,

$$L(q_1, \dots, q_n, \dot{q}_1, \dots, \dot{q}_n, t) = T - V$$

Potential energy

Kinetic energy

Where generally,

$$T(q_1, \dots, q_n, \dot{q}_1, \dots, \dot{q}_n, t) \qquad \text{and}$$

$$V(q_1, \dots, q_n) \text{ - function of positions only(usually)!}$$

q_j -generalized coordinates and $\dot{q}_j$ -generalized velocities

$$j = 1, 2, \dots n; \qquad n - \text{degree of freedom } (n \le 3N)$$

$$L(q_j, \dot{q}_j, t) = T(q_j, \dot{q}_j, t) - V(q_j)$$

Everything about this system is embodied in this scalar function L!

The **Euler-Langange's** equations, or simply **Langange's** equations,

$$\frac{d}{dt}\left(\frac{\partial L}{\partial \dot{q}_j}\right) - \frac{\partial L}{\partial q_j} = 0$$

n- such equations! One equation for each generalized coordinate.

- To define the Largrangian, potential $V(q_1, \dots, q_n)$ must exist, i,e the **forces are conservative.** (*We shall discuss extension to non-conservative forces later!*)
- There is no need to consider constrain forces in Lagrange's formalism
- The form of Lagrange's equations are independent of choice of generalized coordinates chosen.

The recipe of Lagrangian!

I. (a) Recognize, & obtain the **constraint relations**, (b) determine th DOF, and (c) choose appropriate **generalized coordinates**!

II. Write down the **total** kinetic energy T and potential energy V of the **whole system** in terms of the **Cartesian** coordinates, **to begin with!**

$$T = \sum_{i=1}^{N} \frac{1}{2} m_i (\dot{x}_i^2 + \dot{y}_i^2 + \dot{z}_i^2) \qquad \& \qquad V = V(x_i, y_i, z_i) \qquad |\,i = 1, N$$

III. Obtain appropriate transformation equations
(Cartesian $\to$ generalized coordinates) using constraint relations:

$$\begin{aligned} x_i &= x_i\,(q_1, \ldots, q_n,\ t) \\ y_i &= y_i\,(q_1, \ldots, q_n,\ t) \\ z_i &= z_i\,(q_1, \ldots, q_n,\ t) \end{aligned}$$

IV. Convert T and V from Cartesian to suitable **generalized -coordinates** (q_j) and **generalized velocities** $(\dot{q}_j)$ to write L as,

$$L(q_j, \dot{q}_j, t) = T(q_j, \dot{q}_j, t) - V(q_j) \qquad j = 1, n$$

V. Now Apply E-L equations:

$$\frac{d}{dt}\left(\frac{\partial L}{\partial \dot{q}_j}\right) - \frac{\partial L}{\partial q_j} = 0 \qquad for\ each\ j = 1, n!$$

Questions in your mind?

I guess, there are many unanswered questions which are circulating in your mind

(1) What is the origin of Lagrange's equation?

(2) Is there any **proof** on the validity of the method?

(3) Is their any direct correlation of Lagrange's equation with Newton's laws?

(4) How come constraint forces could be "ignored" in Lagrange's formalism?

We shall answer the questions later, for the moment believe me that Lagrange's equations are correct!

Initially we shall discuss, how to easily solve dynamical problems with Lagrangian formalism!

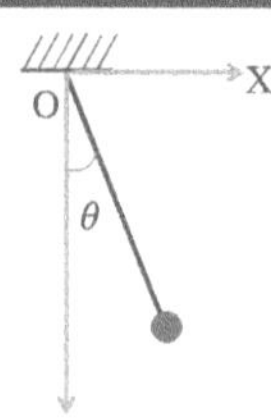

Step-1:
a) Obtain the Constrains relations:

$$z = 0, \qquad\qquad x^2 + y^2 = l^2$$

b) Determine the DOF= 1

c) Choice of generalized coordinate: θ

Step-2: *Write T and V in Cartesian*

Kinetic energy $T = \dfrac{1}{2}m(\dot{x}^2 + \dot{y}^2)$

Potential energy $V = -mgy \qquad$ *(w.r.to "O")*

Step-3: *Identify the transformation relations,* $\quad x = l\,\sin\theta;\; y = l\,\cos\theta$

$$\dot{x} = l\,\cos\theta\,\dot{\theta};\; \dot{y} = -l\,\sin\theta\,\dot{\theta}$$

Example-1 continued….

Step-4: Convert **T** and **V** *to generalized coordinates & velocities using Step3.*

$$T = \frac{1}{2}m\left[\left(l\,\cos\theta\,\dot{\theta}\right)^2 + \left(-l\,\sin\theta\,\dot{\theta}\right)^2\right] = \frac{1}{2}ml^2\dot{\theta}^2$$

$$V = -mgl\,\cos\theta$$

$$L = T - V$$

$$L = \frac{1}{2}ml^2\dot{\theta}^2 + mgl\,\cos\theta$$

Step-5: *Employ Lagrange's equation for each generalized coordinates*

$$\frac{d}{dt}\left(\frac{\partial L}{\partial \dot{q}_j}\right) - \frac{\partial L}{\partial q_j} = 0;\; \textit{in the given problem } q_j = \theta$$

$$\frac{d}{dt}\left(\frac{\partial L}{\partial \dot{\theta}}\right) - \frac{\partial L}{\partial \theta} = 0 \qquad \text{-(1)}$$

$\dfrac{\partial L}{\partial \dot{\theta}} = ml^2\dot{\theta}$ $\qquad$ $\dfrac{d}{dt}\left(\dfrac{\partial L}{\partial \dot{\theta}}\right) = \dfrac{d}{dt}\left(ml^2\dot{\theta}\right) = ml^2\ddot{\theta}$ $\qquad$ $\dfrac{\partial L}{\partial \theta} = -mgl\sin\theta$

$$(1) \Rightarrow \qquad ml^2\ddot{\theta} + mgl\sin\theta = 0 \qquad \textbf{Done!}$$

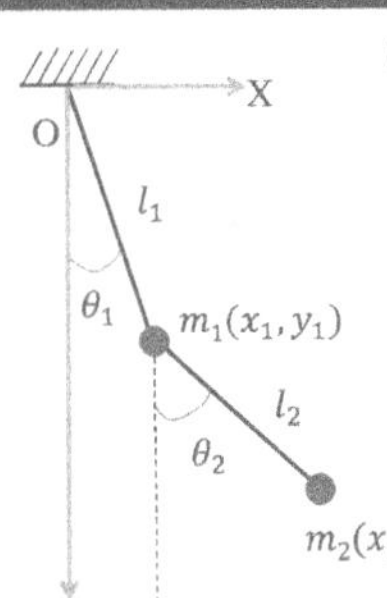

Step-1:

a) Obtain the Constrains relations: $z_1 = 0$; $z_2 = 0$;

$$x_1^{\,2} + y_1^{\,2} = l_1^{\,2}; \quad (x_2 - x_1)^2 + (y_2 - y_1)^2 = l_2^{\,2}$$

b) Determine the DOF= 2

c) Choice of generalized coordinates: θ_1, θ_2

Step-2: *Write the total **T** and total **V** in Cartesian:*

Kinetic energy $T = \frac{1}{2} m_1(\dot{x}_1^{\,2} + \dot{y}_1^{\,2}) + \frac{1}{2} m_2(\dot{x}_2^{\,2} + \dot{y}_2^{\,2})$

Potential energy $V = -m_1 g y_1 - m_2 g y_2$ (*w.r.to "O"*)

Step-3: *Identify the transformation relations:*

$$x_1 = l_1 \sin\theta_1; \quad y_1 = l_1 \cos\theta_1; \quad \dot{x}_1 = l_1 \cos\theta_1\, \dot{\theta}_1; \quad \dot{y}_1 = -l_1 \sin\theta_1\, \dot{\theta}_1$$

$$x_2 = l_1 \sin\theta_1 + l_2 \sin\theta_2; \qquad y_2 = l_1 \cos\theta_1 + l_2 \cos\theta_2;$$

$$\dot{x}_2 = l_1 \cos\theta_1\, \dot{\theta}_1 + l_2 \cos\theta_2\, \dot{\theta}_2; \qquad \dot{y}_2 = -l_1 \sin\theta_1\, \dot{\theta}_1 - l_2 \sin\theta_2\, \dot{\theta}_2$$

Step—4:
Convert **T** and **V** to *generalized coordinates & velocities using Step3.*

$$T = \frac{1}{2} m_1(\dot{x}_1^{\,2} + \dot{y}_1^{\,2}) + \frac{1}{2} m_2(\dot{x}_2^{\,2} + \dot{y}_2^{\,2})$$

$$T = \frac{1}{2} m_1 \left(l_1 \dot{\theta}_1\right)^2 + \frac{1}{2} m_2 \left[\left(l_1 \dot{\theta}_1\right)^2 + \left(l_2 \dot{\theta}_2\right)^2 + 2 l_1 l_2 \dot{\theta}_1 \dot{\theta}_2 \cos(\theta_1 - \theta_2) \right]$$

$$V = -m_1 g y_1 - m_2 g y_2 = -m_1 g l_1 \cos\theta_1 - m_2 g(l_1 \cos\theta_1 + l_2 \cos\theta_2);$$

…continuing **Step–4**: $\qquad L = T - V$

$$L = \frac{1}{2}m_1\left(l_1\dot{\theta}_1\right)^2 + \frac{1}{2}m_2\left[\left(l_1\dot{\theta}_1\right)^2 + \left(l_2\dot{\theta}_2\right)^2 + 2l_1l_2\dot{\theta}_1\dot{\theta}_2\cos(\theta_1 - \theta_2)\right]$$

$$+ m_1gl_1\cos\theta_1 + m_2g(l_1\cos\theta_1 + l_2\cos\theta_2);$$

Step-5: *Employ Lagrange's equation for each generalized coordinates,* θ_1 & θ_2

$$\frac{d}{dt}\left(\frac{\partial L}{\partial \dot{\theta}_1}\right) - \frac{\partial L}{\partial \theta_1} = 0 \quad -[1] \quad \text{and} \quad \frac{d}{dt}\left(\frac{\partial L}{\partial \dot{\theta}_2}\right) - \frac{\partial L}{\partial \theta_2} = 0; \quad -[2]$$

$$\frac{\partial L}{\partial \dot{\theta}_1} = m_1l_1{}^2\dot{\theta}_1 + m_2l_1{}^2\dot{\theta}_1 + m_2\,l_1l_2\dot{\theta}_2\cos(\theta_1 - \theta_2)$$

$$\frac{d}{dt}\left(\frac{\partial L}{\partial \dot{\theta}_1}\right) = m_1l_1{}^2\ddot{\theta}_1 + m_2l_1{}^2\ddot{\theta}_1 + m_2\,l_1l_2\ddot{\theta}_2\cos(\theta_1 - \theta_2) -$$

$$m_2\,l_1l_2\dot{\theta}_2\,(\dot{\theta}_1 - \dot{\theta}_2)\sin(\theta_1 - \theta_2)$$

$$\frac{\partial L}{\partial \theta_1} = -m_2\,l_1l_2\dot{\theta}_1\dot{\theta}_2\sin(\theta_1 - \theta_2) - m_1gl_1\sin\theta_1 - m_2g\,l_1\sin\theta_1$$

So the first E-L equation, $\dfrac{d}{dt}\left(\dfrac{\partial L}{\partial \dot{\theta}_1}\right) - \dfrac{\partial L}{\partial \theta_1} = 0$

$$\Rightarrow \quad m_1l_1{}^2\ddot{\theta}_1 + m_2l_1{}^2\ddot{\theta}_1 +$$
$$m_2\,l_1l_2\ddot{\theta}_2\cos(\theta_1 - \theta_2) - m_2\,l_1l_2\dot{\theta}_2\,(\dot{\theta}_1 - \dot{\theta}_2)\sin(\theta_1 - \theta_2) +$$
$$m_2\,l_1l_2\dot{\theta}_1\dot{\theta}_2\sin(\theta_1 - \theta_2) + m_1gl_1\sin\theta_1 + m_2g\,l_1\sin\theta_1 = 0$$

$$\Rightarrow \quad \boxed{\begin{aligned}&(m_1 + m_2)l_1{}^2\ddot{\theta}_1 + m_2\,l_1l_2\ddot{\theta}_2\cos(\theta_1 - \theta_2) + \\ &m_2\,l_1l_2\dot{\theta}_2{}^2\sin(\theta_1 - \theta_2) + (m_1 + m_2)gl_1\sin\theta_1 = 0\end{aligned}}$$

Similarly, the 2nd E-L equation, $\dfrac{d}{dt}\left(\dfrac{\partial L}{\partial \dot{\theta}_2}\right) - \dfrac{\partial L}{\partial \theta_2} = 0;$

$$\Rightarrow \quad \boxed{\begin{aligned}&m_2\,l_2{}^2\ddot{\theta}_2 + m_2\,l_1l_2\ddot{\theta}_1\cos(\theta_1 - \theta_2) - \\ &m_2\,l_1l_2\dot{\theta}_1{}^2\sin(\theta_1 - \theta_2) + m_2gl_2\sin\theta_2 = 0\end{aligned}}$$

Solved the problem? $\qquad$ **Yes!** As far as **we are concerned**!

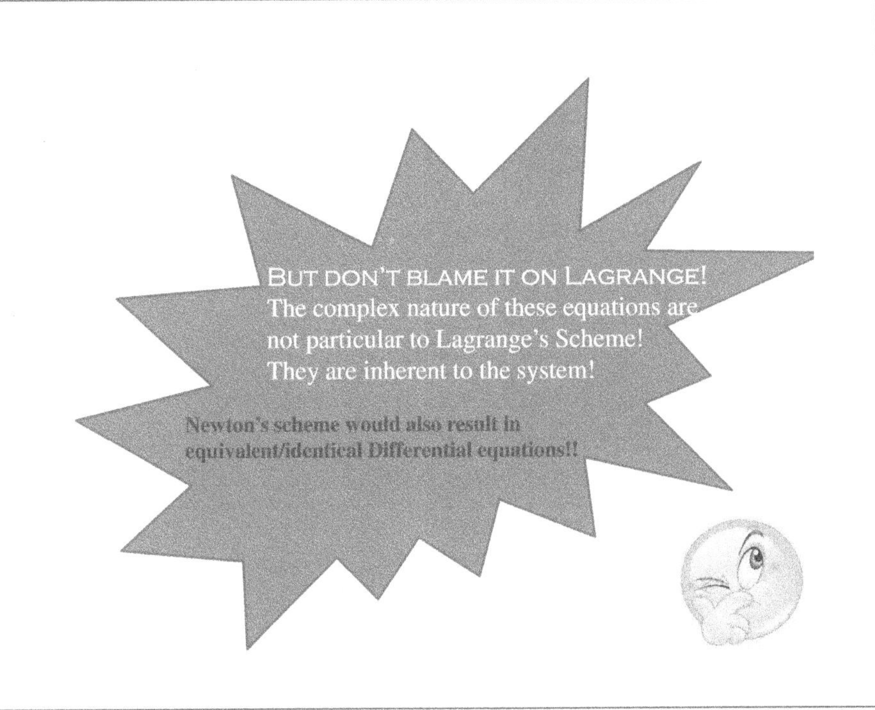

Comments!

Let's first note that: the resulting differential equations are,

a) Second order ($\frac{d^2()}{dt^2}$; -in time)

b) Coupled (such as involving, $\dot{\theta}_1\dot{\theta}_2$) &

c) Non-linear in nature (hence more complex in nature!)

(Linear diff. eq. have the form: $P(x)\frac{d^2y}{dx^2} + Q(x)\frac{dy}{dx} + R(x) = 0$)

Often such equations are very hard to solve!
~~Simple~~ Pendulum for example!

So for **most** problems you may **stop at these E-L (differential-) equations,** say in exams/tutorials!
Unless you are asked **explicitly** to "**solve**" the differential equations! (-only in very simple cases!)

Summery

Choice of generalized coordinates and transformation relations automatically includes constrain relations into the problem.
Thus, Lagrange's formalism does not require to consider constraint forces, rather constraint conditions are smartly utilized. 

Lagrangian $L(q_1, ..., q_n, \dot{q}_1, ..., \dot{q}_n, t) = T - V$, where T and V **SHOULD** be expressed in terms of **generalized** coordinates & velocities, before the E-L equations are invoked/applied!

Largrangian satisfies equations of motion:
$$\frac{d}{dt}\left(\frac{\partial L}{\partial \dot{q}_j}\right) - \frac{\partial L}{\partial q_j} = 0$$
One equation for each generalized coordinate/DOF.

The form of Lagrange's equations are independent of choice of any set of generalized coordinates. (eg., same for r & θ)

What You Should Revise?

- Basic rules of partial differentiation

- Familiarity with different coordinate systems (*Cartesian, Plane polar, Cylindrical, Spherical polar*)

- Conservative forces and potentials

- Motion under constraints:
a) Recognizing and writing down the constraint relations,
b) Determine the degree's of freedom and
c) making proper choice of generalized coordinates (considering also, the **symmetry** of the system).
d) Developing appropriate transformations
   (Cartesian $\rightarrow$ generalized)

Let's cook it! The recipe of Lagrangian!

I. (a) Recognize, & obtain the **constraint relations**, (b) determine the **DOF**, and (c) choose appropriate **generalized coordinates**!

II. Write down the **total** kinetic energy T and potential energy V of the **whole system** in terms of the **Cartesian** coordinates, **to begin with!**

$$T = \sum_{i=1}^{N} \frac{1}{2} m_i(\dot{x}_i^2 + \dot{y}_i^2 + \dot{z}_i^2) \qquad \& \qquad V = V(x_i, y_i, z_i) \qquad | \; i = 1, N$$

III. Obtain appropriate transformation equations
(Cartesian $\rightarrow$ generalized coordinates) using constraint relations:

$$\begin{aligned} x_i &= x_i(q_1, \dots, q_n, t) \\ y_i &= y_i(q_1, \dots, q_n, t) \\ z_i &= z_i(q_1, \dots, q_n, t) \end{aligned}$$

IV. Convert T and V from Cartesian to suitable **generalized -coordinates** (q_j) and **generalized velocities** ($\dot{q}_j$) to write L as,

$$L(q_j, \dot{q}_j, t) = T(q_j, \dot{q}_j, t) - V(q_j) \qquad j = 1, n$$

V. Now Apply E-L equations:

$$\frac{d}{dt}\left(\frac{\partial L}{\partial \dot{q}_j}\right) - \frac{\partial L}{\partial q_j} = 0 \qquad for\ each\ j = 1, n!$$

Lagrange's equations (constraint-free motion)

Before going further let's see the Lagrange's equations recover Newton's 2nd Law, if there are NO constraints!

Let a particle of mass, m, in 3-D motion under a potential, $V(x, y, z)$

If No constraints, then its, DOF=3; Generalized coordinates: (x, y, z)

Now,

$$L = \frac{1}{2} m(\dot{x}^2 + \dot{y}^2 + \dot{z}^2) - V(x, y, z)$$

Corresponding E-L equations are,

$$\frac{d}{dt}\left(\frac{\partial L}{\partial \dot{x}}\right) - \frac{\partial L}{\partial x} = 0$$

$$\left(\frac{\partial L}{\partial \dot{x}}\right) = m\dot{x} = p_x \quad \text{- the x-component of linear momentum!}$$

$$\frac{d}{dt}\left(\frac{\partial L}{\partial \dot{x}}\right) = \frac{dp_x}{dt} \quad \& \quad \frac{\partial L}{\partial x} = -\frac{\partial V}{\partial x} = F_x \quad \text{-the x-component of force!}$$

$$\boxed{F_x = \frac{dp_x}{dt}} \qquad \text{Newton's 2nd Law!}$$

Lagrange's equation: Example 3

Y

A block of mass m is sliding on a wedge of mass M. Wedge can slide on the horizontal table. Find the equation of motion.

X

Initial conditions!

At time t=0: the wedge is stationary and at a distance l from the origin, and the mass m is gently placed at the top point of the Wedge!

Lagrange's equation: Example 3

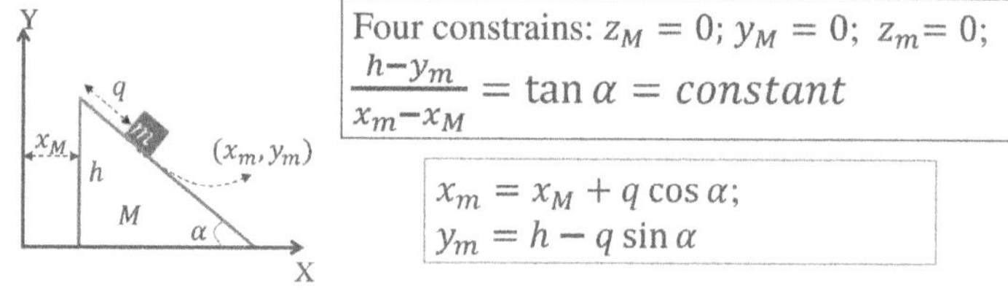

Four constrains: $z_M = 0$; $y_M = 0$; $z_m = 0$;
$$\frac{h - y_m}{x_m - x_M} = \tan \alpha = constant$$

$$x_m = x_M + q \cos \alpha;$$
$$y_m = h - q \sin \alpha$$

Step-1: *Find the degrees of freedom and choose suitable generalized coordinates*

One particle $N = 2$, $no. of\ constrains\ (k) = 4$;
So $DOF = 3 \times 2 - 4 = 2$.

The distance of the wedge from origin (x_M) and distance slipped by the block (q) can serve as generalized coordinates of the system.

Only translation of the given rigid bodies are considered, thus for the calculation of degrees of freedom both of them are considered as point particles.

Step-2: *Find out transformation relations*

$$T = \tfrac{1}{2}m\left(\dot{x}_m{}^2 + \dot{y}_m{}^2\right) + \tfrac{1}{2}M\dot{x}_M{}^2 \; ; \quad V = mgy_m$$

Step-3: *Write T and U in Cartesian*

$$x_m = x_M + q\cos\alpha; \qquad y_m = h - q\sin\alpha$$
$$\dot{x}_m = \dot{x}_M + \dot{q}\cos\alpha; \qquad \dot{y}_m = -\dot{q}\sin\alpha$$

Step-4: Convert *T and V in generalized coordinate using transformations*

$$T = \tfrac{1}{2}m[\dot{x}_M{}^2 + \dot{q}^2 + 2\dot{x}_M\dot{q}\cos\alpha] + \tfrac{1}{2}M\dot{x}_M{}^2;$$
$$V = mg(h - q\sin\alpha)$$

Lagrange's equation: Example 3

Step-5: *Write down Lagrangian*

$$L = T - V$$
$$L = \frac{1}{2}m\left[\dot{x}_M{}^2 + \dot{q}^2 + 2\dot{x}_M\dot{q}\cos\alpha\right] + \frac{1}{2}M\dot{x}_M{}^2 - mg(h - q\sin\alpha)$$

Step-5: *Write down Lagrange's equation for each generalized coordinates*

$$\frac{d}{dt}\left(\frac{\partial L}{\partial \dot{x}_M}\right) - \frac{\partial L}{\partial x_M} = 0; \qquad \frac{d}{dt}\left(\frac{\partial L}{\partial \dot{q}}\right) - \frac{\partial L}{\partial q} = 0$$

From eqn 1

$$\frac{d}{dt}[m\dot{x}_M + m\dot{q}\cos\alpha + M\dot{x}_M] = 0 \qquad \text{----(1)}$$

$$(m + M)\ddot{x}_M + m\ddot{q}\cos\alpha = 0 \qquad \text{----(2)}$$

From eqn 2

$$\frac{d}{dt}[m\dot{q} + m\dot{x}_M\cos\alpha] - [mg\sin\alpha] = 0$$

$$m(\ddot{q} + \ddot{x}_M\cos\alpha) - mg\sin\alpha = 0 \qquad \text{----(3)}$$

$$\frac{\partial L}{\partial \dot{x}_M} = m\dot{x}_M + m\dot{q}\cos\alpha + M\dot{x}_M = \text{constant!} \qquad \text{(from eq (1))}$$

But what's this quantity? | The total linear momentum, say P_x!

So Lagrange's equation tells us that the **total linear momentum is conserved**! We didn't have to **impose** it to solve!

From the Initial conditions given: $x_M = l$, $\dot{x}_M = 0$; $q = 0$; $\dot{q} = 0$
Initial $Px = 0$; So it any other time later!

$$\dot{x}_M = \frac{-m\dot{q}\cos\alpha}{(M+m)} \implies \ddot{x}_M = \frac{-m\ddot{q}\cos\alpha}{(M+m)}$$

This shall be substituted in eq (3): $(\ddot{q} + \ddot{x}_M \cos\alpha) = g\sin\alpha$

And, Solve the problem completely!
(It's left to you to verify with the Newtonian Scheme!)

In some cases further time derivative (such as equation (2)) may not be unnecessary!

Generalized momentum: A few points

Generalized velocity is the rate of charge of generalized coordinate $\dot{q}_j = \dfrac{dq_j}{dt}$

Generalized momentum is not the mass multiplied by generalized velocity.

$$p_j \neq m\dot{q}_j \qquad\qquad p_j = \frac{\partial L}{\partial \dot{q}_j}$$

In specific cases, this relation may be true but it is not the general case.

Definition of **generalized momentum**

Unit/dimension of the generalized momentum depends on generalized coordinate under consideration.

Generalized definition of momentum allows to consider non-mechanical systems, for example EM field. Example: charged particle in EM field $\vec{p} = m\vec{v} + e\vec{A}$

Generalized momentum

Lagrangian of a free particle
$$L = \frac{1}{2}m(\dot{x}^2 + \dot{y}^2 + \dot{z}^2)$$
Thus $\frac{\partial L}{\partial \dot{x}} = m\dot{x}$; now $m\dot{x} \to x$ component of linear momentum (p_x)
$$p_x = m\dot{x} = \frac{\partial L}{\partial \dot{x}} \; ; \text{Similarly, } p_y = \frac{\partial L}{\partial \dot{y}} \text{ and } p_z = \frac{\partial L}{\partial \dot{z}}$$

Lagrangian of a freely rotating wheel with moment of inertia I is
$$L = \frac{1}{2}I\dot{\theta}^2$$
And $\frac{\partial L}{\partial \dot{\theta}} = I\dot{\theta} \to$ Angular momentum

In both the examples, momentum was the derivative of the Lagrangian with respect to generalized velocity.

Generalized momentum associated with generalized coordinate q_j by

$$p_j = \frac{\partial L}{\partial \dot{q}_j}$$

$\longrightarrow$ Also known as conjugate momentum or canonical momentum

Cyclic coordinates

If a particular coordinate does not appear in the Lagrangian, it is called 'Cyclic' or 'Ignorable' coordinate.

Example 1: Lagrangian of a point mass under gravity,
$$L = \frac{1}{2}m(\dot{x}^2 + \dot{y}^2 + \dot{z}^2) - mgz$$
Since neither x nor y appear in the Lagrangian, they are cyclic.
Hence P_x & P_y will be conserved!

Example 2: Lagrangian for a planet of mass m orbiting around the sum (mass M):
$$L = \frac{1}{2}m\left(\dot{r}^2 + r^2\dot{\theta}^2\right) + \frac{GMm}{r}$$

Since θ does not appear in the Lagrangian, it is cyclic coordinate.
Hence $P_\theta = \frac{\partial L}{\partial \dot{\theta}_j} = mr^2\dot{\theta}$ ($\equiv$ **Ang. Momentum!** -will be **conserved!**)

- If there is no explicit dependence of L on generalized coordinate q_j, then

$$\frac{\partial L}{\partial q_j} = 0$$

Thus Lagrange's equation corresponding to cyclic coordinate become,

$$\frac{d}{dt}\left(\frac{\partial L}{\partial \dot{q}_j}\right) = 0 \quad \Rightarrow \quad \frac{dp_j}{dt} = 0$$

Hence, p_j =constant

Generalized momentum conjugate to a cyclic coordinate is a constant

---

Lagrange's equation: Example 4

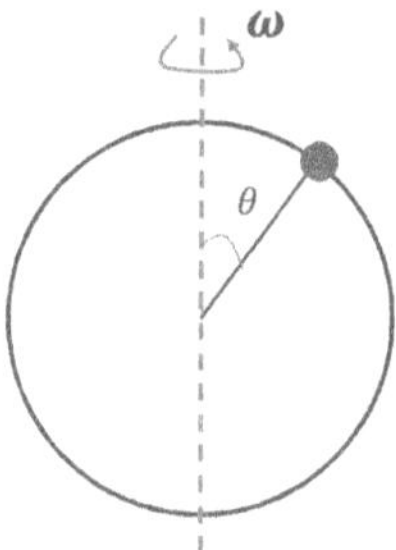

A bead is free to slide along a frictionless hoop of radius R. The hoop rotates with constant angular speed ω around a vertical diameter. Find the equation of motion for the position of the bead.

Lagrange's equation: Example 4

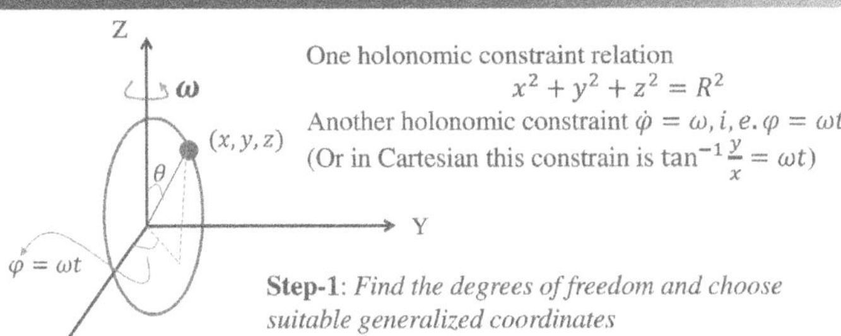

One holonomic constraint relation
$$x^2 + y^2 + z^2 = R^2$$
Another holonomic constraint $\dot\varphi = \omega, i.e.\ \varphi = \omega t$
(Or in Cartesian this constrain is $\tan^{-1}\frac{y}{x} = \omega t$)

Step-1: *Find the degrees of freedom and choose suitable generalized coordinates*

One particle $N = 1,\ no.\ of\ constrains\ (k) = 2$
$$thus\ degrees\ of\ freedom = 3 \times 1 - 2 = 1$$
Hence number of generalized coordinates must be one.

Choice of Generalized coordinate: 'θ' , which the angle of particle with rotation axis (z-axis) of hoop.

Lagrange's equation: Example 4

Step-2: *Find out transformation relations*

$$x = R \sin\theta \cos\omega t\ ; y = R \sin\theta \sin\omega t\ ; z = R \cos\theta$$

$$\dot{x} = R \cos\theta \cos\omega t\ \dot\theta - R\ \omega\sin\theta \sin\omega t$$
$$\dot{y} = R \cos\theta \sin\omega t\ \dot\theta + R\omega \sin\theta \cos\omega t$$
$$\dot{z} = -R \sin\theta\ \dot\theta$$

Step-3: *Write T and V in Cartesian*

$$T = \frac{1}{2}m(\dot{x}^2 + \dot{y}^2 + \dot{z}^2);\quad \&\quad V = mgz$$

Step-4:Convert *T and V to generalized coordinate , either using,*
(a) transformation at Step#2 Or,
(b) in this case employing spherical polar equations.

$$T = \frac{1}{2}m[R^2\dot\theta^2 + R^2\omega^2 sin^2\theta];$$
$$V = mgR \cos\theta$$

Step-5: *Write down Lagrangian*

$$L = T - V$$
$$L = \frac{1}{2}m\left[R^2\dot{\theta}^2 + R^2\omega^2 \sin^2\theta\right] - mgR\cos\theta$$

Step-5: *Lagrange's equation*

$$\frac{d}{dt}\left(\frac{\partial L}{\partial \dot{\theta}}\right) - \frac{\partial L}{\partial \theta} = 0$$

$$\frac{\partial L}{\partial \dot{\theta}} = mR^2\dot{\theta} \quad \& \quad \frac{\partial L}{\partial \theta} = mR^2\omega^2 \sin\theta \cos\theta + mgR\sin\theta$$

$$\frac{d}{dt}\left[mR^2\dot{\theta}\right] - \left[mR^2\omega^2 \sin\theta \cos\theta + mgR\sin\theta\right] = 0$$

$$mR^2\ddot{\theta} - \left[mR^2\omega^2 \sin\theta \cos\theta + mgR\sin\theta\right] = 0$$

Example-5

A mass M slides down a frictionless plane inclined at angle α. A pendulum, with length l, and mass m, is attached to M. Find the equations of motion.

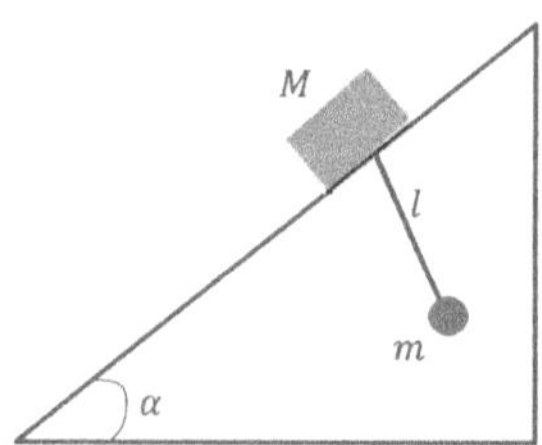

Simple pendulum with a variable string length $l(t)$
[Time dependent constraint]

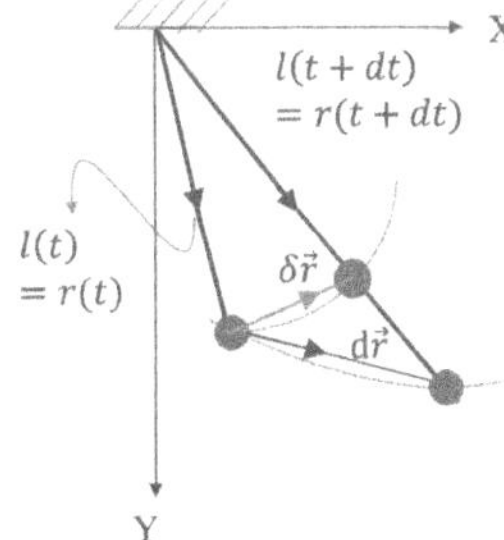

Real displacement of the bob in time dt is given by
$$d\vec{r} = \vec{r}(t + dt) - \vec{r}(t)$$

Let's **imagine** any **instantaneous arbitrary displacement** at time t (that is, *without allowing time to change, $dt = 0$*) AND **consistent with the constraint relations at time t**?

Imaginary, instantaneous displacement which is consistent with the constrain relation at a given instant (i,e. without allowing real time to change) is called *Virtual displacement* and denoted by $\delta\vec{r}$ (for infinitesimal case)

- By definition a virtual infinitesimal displacement is given by

$$\delta x_i = dx_i\Big|_{dt = 0}$$

- If the constraint is not time dependent, the real and virtual displacements matches each other.

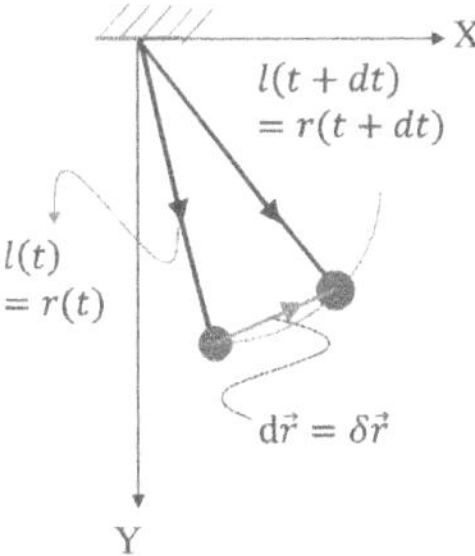

Virtual displacement in generalized coordinates

❑ Consider a system of N particles with k constrains, DOF, $n = 3N - k$

❑ Cartesian coordinates, $\vec{r}_i = \vec{r}_i (x_1, y_1, z_1, \ldots x_N, y_N, z_N) \mid (i = 1, \ldots \ldots, N)$

❑ Generalized coordinates $q_j \quad \mid (j = 1, \ldots.., n)$

❑ Virtual displacements of the particles $\delta\vec{r}_1, \delta\vec{r}_2, \ldots.., \delta\vec{r}_N$

❑ Virtual displacements of the particles in the generalized coordinates $\delta q_1, \delta q_2, \ldots.., \delta q_n$ can be found from given transformation relations

$$\vec{r}_1 = \vec{r}_1(q_1, q_2, \ldots., q_n, t)$$
$$\vec{r}_2 = \vec{r}_2(q_1, q_2, \ldots., q_n, t)$$
$$\cdots\cdots\cdots\cdots\cdots\cdots\cdots$$
$$\vec{r}_N = \vec{r}_N(q_1, q_2, \ldots., q_n, t)$$

$$\delta\vec{r}_i = \sum_{j=1}^{n} \frac{\partial \vec{r}_i}{\partial q_j} \delta q_j$$

$3N$ coordinates, not independent

$n = 3N - k$ generalized coordinates, independent

Note: There is no $\frac{\partial \vec{r}_i}{\partial t}\delta t$, as virtual displacement is instantaneous without allowing time to change, $\delta t{=}0$

Virtual work done

Real work done: Work done due to real displacement ($d\vec{r}$) of a particle acted on by total force $\vec{F}$ is given by

$$dW = \vec{F}.d\vec{r}$$

As you can always **imagine** an instantaneous displacement (without allowing time to change), known as virtual displacement ($\delta\vec{r}$), and hence you can always define a scalar function

$$\delta W = \vec{F}.\delta\vec{r}$$

This scalar function is know called **Virtual work done.**

Note: 'Virtual work' is different from 'Real work', as virtual displacement is imagined without allowing time to change.

Consider a system of particles and $\vec{F}_1, \vec{F}_2, \ldots, \vec{F}_N$ are the forces on $1,2 \ldots N_{th}$ particles, then

Total virtual work done

$$\delta W = \sum_{i=1}^{N} \vec{F}_i . \delta \vec{r}_i$$

Here, force on each particle, $\vec{F}_i$ is the sum of external force and also forces of constraints.

$$\vec{F}_i = \vec{F}_{ie} + \vec{f}_{ic}$$

Where,

$\vec{F}_{ie}$ is the external applied force on i_{th} particle.

$\vec{f}_{ic}$ is the constraint force

Newton's second law reads as

$$m\ddot{\vec{r}} = \vec{F}$$

Total force$(\vec{F})$ = Applied force$(\vec{F}_e)$ + constraint force $(\vec{f}_c)$

$$m\ddot{\vec{r}} = \vec{F}_e + \vec{f}_c$$

Taking dot product with an infinitesimal virtual displacement $\delta \vec{r}$

$$m\ddot{\vec{r}} \cdot \delta \vec{r} = (\vec{F}_e + \vec{f}_c) \cdot \delta \vec{r} \quad\boxed{1}$$

Now, virtual displacement is instantaneous (frozen in time & imaginary) AND **consistent with ALL the constraint relations.**

As $\delta \vec{r}$ are perpendicular to $\vec{f}_c$, thus virtual work due to constraint force is zero, $\vec{f}_c \cdot \delta \vec{r} = 0$

If virtual work done by the constraint forces is ($\vec{f}_c \cdot \delta\vec{r} = 0$) (from eq.-1),

$$\left(\vec{F}_e - m\ddot{\vec{r}}\right) \cdot \delta\vec{r} = 0 \longrightarrow \text{D'Alembert's principle of Virtual work}$$

Now, for a general system of N particles having virtual displacements, $\delta\vec{r}_1, \delta\vec{r}_2, \ldots, \delta\vec{r}_N$,

$$\sum_{i=1}^{N}\left(\vec{F}_{ie} - m_i\ddot{\vec{r}}_i\right) \cdot \delta\vec{r}_i = 0 \qquad \vec{F}_{ie} \to \text{Applied force on } i_{th} \text{ particle}$$

Does not necessarily means that individual terms of the summation are zero as $\vec{r}_i$ are not independent, they are connected by constrain relation

---

Lagrange's equation from D'Alembert's principle

$$\sum_{i=1}^{N}\left(\vec{F}_{ie} - m_i\ddot{\vec{r}}_i\right) \cdot \delta\vec{r}_i = 0$$

❑ Want to express this relation in such a way where all the terms in the summation becomes individually zero.

how to do?

Let's remember:
$u_1\,\delta x_1 + u_2\,\delta x_2 = 0$; does this always mean $u_1 = 0$ and $u_2 = 0$?

If x_1 and x_2 are independent then $u_1 = 0$ and $u_2 = 0$ for all possible variation of x_1 and x_2,

If x_1 and x_2 are not independent, changing one will change the other.

$\sum u_i\,\delta x_i = 0, then\ all\ u_i$ will be individually zero for all possible variation of the x_i if they are independent.

❏ D'Alembert's principle,

$$\sum_{i=1}^{N}(\vec{F}_{ie} - m_i\ddot{\vec{r}}_i)\cdot\delta\vec{r}_i = 0$$

Constraint forces are out of the game!

Now, no need of additional subscript, we shall simply write $\vec{F}_i$ instead of $\vec{F}_{ie}$

But How to express this relation so that individual terms in the summation are zero?

Switch to generalized coordinate system as they are independent!

Let's take the 1st term

$$\sum_{i}\vec{F}_i\cdot\delta\vec{r}_i = \sum_{i}\vec{F}_i\cdot\sum_{j=1}^{n}\frac{\partial\vec{r}_i}{\partial q_j}\delta q_j = \sum_{j=1}^{n}\left(\sum_{i}\vec{F}_i\cdot\frac{\partial\vec{r}_i}{\partial q_j}\right)\delta q_j = \sum_{j=1}^{n}Q_j\delta q_j$$

$$Q_j = \sum_{i}\vec{F}_i\cdot\frac{\partial\vec{r}_i}{\partial q_j} \longrightarrow \text{Generalized force}$$

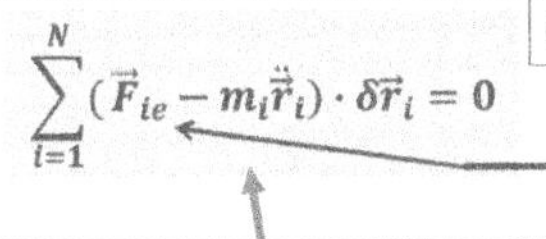

❏ Dimensions of Q_j is **not** always of force!
❏ Dimensions of $Q_j\delta q_j$ is always of work!

Lagrange's equation from D'Alembert's principle

❏ 2nd Term:

$$\sum_{i}m_i\ddot{\vec{r}}_i\cdot\delta\vec{r}_i = \sum_{i}m_i\ddot{\vec{r}}_i\cdot\sum_{j=1}^{n}\frac{\partial\vec{r}_i}{\partial q_j}\delta q_j = \sum_{i,j}m_i\ddot{\vec{r}}_i\cdot\frac{\partial\vec{r}_i}{\partial q_j}\delta q_j$$

❏ Bit of rearrangement in derivatives

$$\ddot{\vec{r}}_i\cdot\frac{\partial\vec{r}_i}{\partial q_j} = \frac{d}{dt}\left(\dot{\vec{r}}_i\cdot\frac{\partial\vec{r}_i}{\partial q_j}\right) - \dot{\vec{r}}_i\cdot\frac{d}{dt}\left(\frac{\partial\vec{r}_i}{\partial q_j}\right)$$

Time and coordinate derivative can be interchanged!

$$= \frac{d}{dt}\left(\dot{\vec{r}}_i\cdot\frac{\partial\dot{\vec{r}}_i}{\partial\dot{q}_j}\right) - \dot{\vec{r}}_i\cdot\left(\frac{\partial\dot{\vec{r}}_i}{\partial q_j}\right)$$

$$\frac{d}{dt}\left(\frac{\partial\vec{r}_i}{\partial q_j}\right) = \left(\frac{\partial\dot{\vec{r}}_i}{\partial q_j}\right)$$

dot cancellation!

$$\frac{\partial\vec{r}_i}{\partial q_j} = \frac{\partial\dot{\vec{r}}_i}{\partial\dot{q}_j}$$

$$= \frac{d}{dt}\left\{\frac{\partial}{\partial\dot{q}_j}\left(\frac{1}{2}\dot{r}_i^{\,2}\right)\right\} - \frac{\partial}{\partial q_j}\left(\frac{1}{2}\dot{r}_i^{\,2}\right)$$

Interchange of order of differential operators

$$\vec{r}_i = \vec{r}_i(q_1, \ldots, q_n, t)$$

$$\boxed{\frac{d}{dt}\left(\frac{\partial \vec{r}_i}{\partial q_j}\right) = \frac{\partial \dot{\vec{r}}_i}{\partial q_j}} \qquad \frac{\partial \vec{r}_i}{\partial q_j} = \frac{\partial \vec{r}_i}{\partial q_j}(q_1, \ldots q_n; t)$$

$$\dot{\vec{r}}_i = \frac{d\vec{r}_i}{dt} = \frac{\partial \vec{r}_i}{\partial q_1}\dot{q}_1 + \frac{\partial \vec{r}_i}{\partial q_2}\dot{q}_2 + \ldots + \frac{\partial \vec{r}_i}{\partial q_n}\dot{q}_n + \frac{\partial \vec{r}_i}{\partial t}$$

$$\text{RHS} = \frac{\partial \dot{\vec{r}}_i}{\partial q_j} = \frac{\partial^2 \vec{r}_i}{\partial q_j \partial q_1}\dot{q}_1 + \frac{\partial^2 \vec{r}_i}{\partial q_j \partial q_2}\dot{q}_2 + \ldots + \frac{\partial^2 \vec{r}_i}{\partial q_j \partial q_n}\dot{q}_n + \frac{\partial^2 \vec{r}_i}{\partial q_j \partial t}$$

$$\text{LHS} = \frac{d}{dt}\left(\frac{\partial \vec{r}_i}{\partial q_j}\right) = \frac{\partial}{\partial q_1}\left(\frac{\partial \vec{r}_i}{\partial q_j}\right)\frac{dq_1}{dt} + \cdots + \frac{\partial}{\partial q_n}\left(\frac{\partial \vec{r}_i}{\partial q_j}\right)\frac{dq_n}{dt} + \frac{\partial}{\partial t}\left(\frac{\partial \vec{r}_i}{\partial q_j}\right)$$

$$= \frac{\partial^2 \vec{r}_i}{\partial q_j \partial q_1}\dot{q}_1 + \frac{\partial^2 \vec{r}_i}{\partial q_j \partial q_2}\dot{q}_2 + \ldots + \frac{\partial^2 \vec{r}_i}{\partial q_j \partial q_n}\dot{q}_n + \frac{\partial^2 \vec{r}_i}{\partial q_j \partial t} = \text{RHS}$$

$$\boxed{\frac{\partial^2 V}{\partial x \partial y} = \frac{\partial^2 V}{\partial y \partial x}}$$

This true for any x & y!
ie., even if say, $y = t$!

Interchange of order of differential operators

$$\frac{\partial \vec{r}_i}{\partial q_j} = \frac{\partial \dot{\vec{r}}_i}{\partial \dot{q}_j}$$

$$\dot{\vec{r}}_i = \dot{\vec{r}}_i(q_1, \ldots q_n; \dot{q}_1, \ldots \dot{q}_2; t)$$

$$\dot{\vec{r}}_i = \frac{d\vec{r}_i}{dt} = \frac{\partial \vec{r}_i}{\partial q_1}\dot{q}_1 + \frac{\partial \vec{r}_i}{\partial q_2}\dot{q}_2 + \cdots + \frac{\partial \vec{r}_i}{\partial q_j}\dot{q}_j + \cdots + \frac{\partial \vec{r}_i}{\partial q_n}\dot{q}_n + \frac{\partial \vec{r}_i}{\partial t}$$

Let's look at the dependency=> $\quad \dfrac{\partial \vec{r}_i}{\partial q_j} = \dfrac{\partial \vec{r}_i}{\partial q_j}(q_1, \ldots q_n; t)$

$$\text{RHS} = \quad \frac{\partial \dot{\vec{r}}_i}{\partial \dot{q}_j} = \frac{\partial \vec{r}_i}{\partial q_j} \quad = \text{LHS}$$

Lagrange's equation from D'Alembert's principle

❑ Thus 2nd term becomes

$$\sum_{i=1}^{N} m_i \ddot{\vec{r}}_i \cdot \delta \vec{r}_i = \sum_{i,j} m_i \left[\frac{d}{dt}\left\{ \frac{d}{d\dot{q}_j}\left(\frac{1}{2}\dot{r}_i^{\,2} \right) \right\} - \frac{\partial}{\partial q_j}\left(\frac{1}{2}\dot{r}_i^{\,2} \right) \right] \delta q_j$$

$$= \sum_{j} \left[\frac{d}{dt}\left\{ \frac{\partial}{\partial \dot{q}_j}\left(\sum_i \frac{1}{2} m_i \dot{r}_i^{\,2} \right) \right\} - \frac{\partial}{\partial q_j}\left(\sum_i \frac{1}{2} m_i \dot{r}_i^{\,2} \right) \right] \delta q_j$$

$$= \sum_{j} \left\{ \frac{d}{dt}\left(\frac{\partial T}{\partial \dot{q}_i} \right) - \frac{\partial T}{\partial q_j} \right\} \delta q_j$$

The 1st term

$$\sum_{i} \vec{F}_i \cdot \delta \vec{r}_i = \sum_{j=1}^{n} Q_j \delta q_j$$

Lagrange's equation from D'Alembert's principle

❑ D'Alembert's principle in generalized coordinates becomes

$$\sum_{j} \left\{ \frac{d}{dt}\left(\frac{\partial T}{\partial \dot{q}_j} \right) - \frac{\partial T}{\partial q_j} \right\} \delta q_j = \sum_{j} Q_j \delta q_j$$

$$\sum_{j} \left[\left\{ \frac{d}{dt}\left(\frac{\partial T}{\partial \dot{q}_j} \right) - \frac{\partial T}{\partial q_j} \right\} - Q_j \right] \delta q_j = 0$$

Well, we are very close to Lagrange's equation!

❑ Since generalized coordinates q_j are all independent each term in the summation is zero

$$\frac{d}{dt}\left(\frac{\partial T}{\partial \dot{q}_j} \right) - \frac{\partial T}{\partial q_j} = Q_j$$

$$-\left(\frac{\partial V_i}{\partial x_i}\hat{\imath} + \frac{\partial V_i}{\partial y_i}\hat{\jmath} + \frac{\partial V_i}{\partial z_i}\hat{k} \right) \cdot \left(\frac{\partial x_i}{\partial q_j}\hat{\imath} + \frac{\partial y_i}{\partial q_j}\hat{\jmath} + \frac{\partial z_i}{\partial q_j}\hat{k} \right)$$

$$= -\left(\frac{\partial V_i}{\partial x_i}\frac{\partial x_i}{\partial q_j} + \frac{\partial V_i}{\partial y_i}\frac{\partial y_i}{\partial q_j} + \frac{\partial V_i}{\partial z_i}\frac{\partial z_i}{\partial q_j} \right)$$

❑ If all the forces are conservative, then $\vec{F}_i = -\vec{\nabla} V_i$

$$Q_j = \sum_{i}(-\vec{\nabla}V_i) \cdot \frac{\partial \vec{r}_i}{\partial q_j} = -\sum_{i} \frac{\partial V_i}{\partial q_j} = -\frac{\partial}{\partial q_j}\sum_{i} V_i = -\frac{\partial V}{\partial q_j}$$

Total potential

$$V = \sum_{i} V_i$$

Lagrange's equation from D'Alembert's principle

Hence,
$$\frac{d}{dt}\left(\frac{\partial T}{\partial \dot{q}_j}\right) - \frac{\partial T}{\partial q_j} = Q_j = -\frac{\partial V}{\partial q_j}$$

❑ Assume that **V does not depend on $\dot{q}_j$**, then $\dfrac{\partial V}{\partial \dot{q}_j} = 0$

$$\frac{d}{dt}\left\{\frac{\partial}{\partial \dot{q}_j}(T - V)\right\} - \frac{\partial(T - V)}{\partial q_j} = 0$$

$$\frac{d}{dt}\left(\frac{\partial L}{\partial \dot{q}_j}\right) - \frac{\partial L}{\partial q_j} = 0$$

Where,
$$L(q_j, \dot{q}_j, t) = T(q_j, \dot{q}_j, t) - V(q_j, t)$$

We have reached to Lagrange's equation from D'Alembert's principle.

Review of the steps we followed

❑ Started from Newton's law
$$m\ddot{\vec{r}} = \vec{F}_e + \vec{f}_c$$

❑ Taken dot product with virtual displacement to kick out constrain force from the game by using $\vec{f}_c \cdot \delta\vec{r} = 0$; Arrive at D'Alembert's principle $\left(\vec{F}_e - m\ddot{\vec{r}} \cdot \delta\vec{r}\right) \cdot \delta\vec{r} = 0$

❑ Extended D'Alembert's principle for a system of particles;
$$\sum_{i=1}^{N}(\vec{F}_{ie} - m_i\ddot{\vec{r}}_i) \cdot \delta\vec{r}_i = 0$$

❑ Converted this expression in generalized coordinate system that *"every"* term of this summation is zero to get

$$\frac{d}{dt}\left(\frac{\partial T}{\partial \dot{q}_i}\right) - \frac{\partial T}{\partial q_j} = Q_j \qquad$$ **This is a more general expression!**

❑ Now, with the assumptions: i) Forces are conservative, $\vec{F}_i = -\vec{\nabla}V_i$, hence $Q_j = -\dfrac{\partial V}{\partial q_j}$ and ii) potential does not depend on $\dot{q}_j$, then $\dfrac{\partial V}{\partial \dot{q}_j} = 0$

We get back our Lagrange's eqn., $\qquad \dfrac{d}{dt}\left(\dfrac{\partial L}{\partial \dot{q}_j}\right) - \dfrac{\partial L}{\partial q_j} = 0$

D'Alembert's principle of virtual work

If virtual work done by the constraint forces is ($\vec{f}_c \cdot \delta\vec{r} = 0$) (from eq.-1),

$$\left(\vec{F}_e - m\ddot{\vec{r}}\right) \cdot \delta\vec{r} = 0 \quad \longrightarrow \quad \text{D'Alembert's principle of Virtual work}$$

Now, for a general system of N particles having virtual displacements, $\delta\vec{r}_1, \delta\vec{r}_2, \ldots, \delta\vec{r}_N$,

$$\sum_{i=1}^{N} \left(\vec{F}_{ie} - m_i\ddot{\vec{r}}_i\right) \cdot \delta\vec{r}_i = 0 \qquad \vec{F}_{ie} \rightarrow \text{Applied force on } i_{th} \text{ particle}$$

Does not necessarily means that individual terms of the summation are zero as $\vec{r}_i$ are not independent, they are connected by constrain relation

Lagrange's equation from D'Alembert's principle

❑ D'Alembert's principle,

$$\sum_{i=1}^{N} \left(\vec{F}_{ie} - m_i\ddot{\vec{r}}_i\right) \cdot \delta\vec{r}_i = 0$$

Constraint forces are out of the game!

Now, no need of additional subscript, we shall simply write $\vec{F}_i$ instead of $\vec{F}_{ie}$

But How to express this relation so that individual terms in the summation are zero?

Switch to generalized coordinate system as they are independent!

Let's take the 1st term

$$\sum_i \vec{F}_i \cdot \delta\vec{r}_i = \sum_i \vec{F}_i \cdot \sum_{j=1}^{n} \frac{\partial\vec{r}_i}{\partial q_j} \delta q_j = \sum_{j=1}^{n} \left(\sum_i \vec{F}_i \cdot \frac{\partial\vec{r}_i}{\partial q_j}\right) \delta q_j = \sum_{j=1}^{n} Q_j \delta q_j$$

$$Q_j = \sum_i \vec{F}_i \cdot \frac{\partial\vec{r}_i}{\partial q_j} \quad \longrightarrow \quad \text{Generalized force}$$

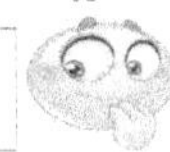

❑ Dimensions of Q_j is **not** always of force!
❑ Dimensions of $Q_j \delta q_j$ is always of work!

❑ 2nd Term:

$$\sum_i m_i \ddot{\vec{r}_i} \cdot \delta \vec{r}_i = \sum_i m_i \ddot{\vec{r}_i} \cdot \sum_{j=1}^{n} \frac{\partial \vec{r}_i}{\partial q_j} \delta q_j = \sum_{i,j} m_i \ddot{\vec{r}_i} \cdot \frac{\partial \vec{r}_i}{\partial q_j} \delta q_j$$

❑ Bit of rearrangement in derivatives

$$\ddot{\vec{r}_i} \cdot \frac{\partial \vec{r}_i}{\partial q_j} = \frac{d}{dt}\left(\dot{\vec{r}_i} \cdot \frac{\partial \vec{r}_i}{\partial q_j} \right) - \dot{\vec{r}_i} \cdot \frac{d}{dt}\left(\frac{\partial \vec{r}_i}{\partial q_j} \right)$$

$$= \frac{d}{dt}\left(\dot{\vec{r}_i} \cdot \frac{\partial \dot{\vec{r}_i}}{\partial q_j} \right) - \dot{\vec{r}_i} \cdot \left(\frac{\partial \dot{\vec{r}_i}}{\partial q_j} \right)$$

Time and coordinate derivative can be interchanged!

$$\frac{d}{dt}\left(\frac{\partial \vec{r}_i}{\partial q_j} \right) = \left(\frac{\partial \dot{\vec{r}_i}}{\partial q_j} \right)$$

dot cancellation!

$$\frac{\partial \vec{r}_i}{\partial q_j} = \frac{\partial \dot{\vec{r}_i}}{\partial \dot{q}_j}$$

$$= \frac{d}{dt}\left\{ \frac{\partial}{\partial \dot{q}_j}\left(\frac{1}{2}\dot{r}_i^{\,2} \right) \right\} - \frac{\partial}{\partial q_j}\left(\frac{1}{2}\dot{r}_i^{\,2} \right)$$

❑ Thus 2nd term becomes

$$\sum_{i=1}^{N} m_i \ddot{\vec{r}_i} \cdot \delta \vec{r}_i = \sum_{i,j} m_i \left[\frac{d}{dt}\left\{ \frac{d}{d\dot{q}_j}\left(\frac{1}{2}\dot{r}_i^{\,2} \right) \right\} - \frac{\partial}{\partial q_j}\left(\frac{1}{2}\dot{r}_i^{\,2} \right) \right] \delta q_j$$

$$= \sum_j \left[\frac{d}{dt}\left\{ \frac{\partial}{\partial \dot{q}_j}\left(\sum_i \frac{1}{2}m_i\dot{r}_i^{\,2} \right) \right\} - \frac{\partial}{\partial q_j}\left(\sum_i \frac{1}{2}m_i\dot{r}_i^{\,2} \right) \right] \delta q_j$$

$$= \sum_j \left\{ \frac{d}{dt}\left(\frac{\partial T}{\partial \dot{q}_i} \right) - \frac{\partial T}{\partial q_j} \right\} \delta q_j$$

The 1st term

$$\sum_i \vec{F}_i \cdot \delta \vec{r}_i = \sum_{j=1}^{n} Q_j \delta q_j$$

Lagrange's equation from D'Alembert's principle

$$\sum_j \left\{ \frac{d}{dt}\left(\frac{\partial T}{\partial \dot{q}_j}\right) - \frac{\partial T}{\partial q_j} \right\} \delta q_j = \sum_j Q_j \delta q_j$$

$$\sum_j \left[\left\{ \frac{d}{dt}\left(\frac{\partial T}{\partial \dot{q}_j}\right) - \frac{\partial T}{\partial q_j} \right\} - Q_j \right] \delta q_j = 0$$

Well, we are very close to Lagrange's equation!

❏ Since generalized coordinates q_j are all independent each term in the summation is zero

$$\frac{d}{dt}\left(\frac{\partial T}{\partial \dot{q}_j}\right) - \frac{\partial T}{\partial q_j} = Q_j$$

$$-\left(\frac{\partial V_i}{\partial x_i}\hat{\imath} + \frac{\partial V_i}{\partial y_i}\hat{\jmath} + \frac{\partial V_i}{\partial z_i}\hat{k}\right) \cdot \left(\frac{\partial x_i}{\partial q_j}\hat{\imath} + \frac{\partial y_i}{\partial q_j}\hat{\jmath} + \frac{\partial z_i}{\partial q_j}\hat{k}\right)$$

$$= -\left(\frac{\partial V_i}{\partial x_i}\frac{\partial x_i}{\partial q_j} + \frac{\partial V_i}{\partial y_i}\frac{\partial y_i}{\partial q_j} + \frac{\partial V_i}{\partial z_i}\frac{\partial z_i}{\partial q_j}\right)$$

❏ If all the forces are conservative, then $\vec{F}_i = -\vec{\nabla} V_i$

$$Q_j = \sum_i (-\vec{\nabla} V_i) \cdot \frac{\partial \vec{r}_i}{\partial q_j} = -\sum_i \frac{\partial V_i}{\partial q_j} = -\frac{\partial}{\partial q_j}\sum_i V_i = -\frac{\partial V}{\partial q_j}$$

Total potential

$$V = \sum_i V_i$$

Lagrange's equation from D'Alembert's principle

Hence,

$$\frac{d}{dt}\left(\frac{\partial T}{\partial \dot{q}_j}\right) - \frac{\partial T}{\partial q_j} = Q_j = -\frac{\partial V}{\partial q_j}$$

❏ Assume that **V does not depend on $\dot{q}_j$**, then $\dfrac{\partial V}{\partial \dot{q}_j} = 0$

$$\frac{d}{dt}\left\{ \frac{\partial}{\partial \dot{q}_j}(T - V) \right\} - \frac{\partial(T - V)}{\partial q_j} = 0$$

$$\frac{d}{dt}\left(\frac{\partial L}{\partial \dot{q}_j}\right) - \frac{\partial L}{\partial q_j} = 0$$

Where,
$$L(q_j, \dot{q}_j, t) = T(q_j, \dot{q}_j, t) - V(q_j, t)$$

We have reached to Lagrange's equation from D'Alembert's principle.

❑ Started from Newton's law

$$m\ddot{\vec{r}} = \vec{F}_e + \vec{f}_c$$

❑ Taken dot product with virtual displacement to kick out constrain force from the game by using $\vec{f}_c \cdot \delta\vec{r} = 0$; Arrive at D'Alembert's principle $\left(\vec{F}_e - m\ddot{\vec{r}} \cdot \delta\vec{r}\right) \cdot \delta\vec{r} = 0$

❑ Extended D'Alembert's principle for a system of particles;

$$\sum_{i=1}^{N} (\vec{F}_{ie} - m_i\ddot{\vec{r}}_i) \cdot \delta\vec{r}_i = 0$$

❑ Converted this expression in generalized coordinate system that *"every"* term of this summation is zero to get

$$\frac{d}{dt}\left(\frac{\partial T}{\partial \dot{q}_i}\right) - \frac{\partial T}{\partial q_j} = Q_j$$

This is a more general expression!

❑ Now, with the assumptions: i) Forces are conservative, $\vec{F}_i = -\vec{\nabla}V_i$, hence $Q_j = -\frac{\partial V}{\partial q_j}$ and ii) potential does not depend on $\dot{q}_j$, then $\frac{\partial V}{\partial \dot{q}_j} = 0$

We get back our Lagrange's eqn.,

$$\frac{d}{dt}\left(\frac{\partial L}{\partial \dot{q}_j}\right) - \frac{\partial L}{\partial q_j} = 0$$

❑ A system may experience both conservative, non-conservative forces

i,e. $\vec{F}_i = \vec{F}_i^{\,c} + \vec{F}_i^{\,nc}$

❑ Hence generalized force for the system

$$Q_j = \sum_i \vec{F}_i \cdot \frac{\partial \vec{r}_i}{\partial q_j} = \sum_i \left(\vec{F}_i^{\,c} + \vec{F}_i^{\,nc}\right) \cdot \frac{\partial \vec{r}_i}{\partial q_j} = \sum_i \vec{F}_i^{\,c} \cdot \frac{\partial \vec{r}_i}{\partial q_j} + \sum_i \vec{F}_i^{\,nc} \cdot \frac{\partial \vec{r}_i}{\partial q_j}$$

$$Q_j = Q_j^{\,c} + Q_j^{\,nc}$$

$$Q_j^{\,c} = \sum_i \vec{F}_i^{\,c} \cdot \frac{\partial \vec{r}_i}{\partial q_j} \quad \Rightarrow$$

❑ Generalized force corresponding to conservative part

$$Q_j^{\,nc} = \sum_i \vec{F}_i^{\,nc} \cdot \frac{\partial \vec{r}_i}{\partial q_j} \quad \Rightarrow$$

❑ Generalized force corresponding to non-conservative part

❑ If system may experience both conservative, non-conservative forces

$$\frac{d}{dt}\left(\frac{\partial T}{\partial \dot{q}_i}\right) - \frac{\partial T}{\partial q_j} = Q_j{}^c + Q_j{}^{nc}$$

❑ Generalized force corresponding to conservative force can be derived from potential $Q_j{}^c = -\dfrac{\partial V}{\partial q_j}$

$$\frac{d}{dt}\left(\frac{\partial T}{\partial \dot{q}_i}\right) - \frac{\partial T}{\partial q_j} = -\frac{\partial V}{\partial q_j} + Q_j{}^{nc}$$

$$\frac{d}{dt}\left\{\frac{\partial}{\partial \dot{q}_j}(T-V)\right\} - \frac{\partial(T-V)}{\partial q_j} = Q_j{}^{nc}$$

❑ Assume that V does not depend on $\dot{q}_j$, then $\dfrac{\partial V}{\partial \dot{q}_j} = 0$

$$\frac{d}{dt}\left(\frac{\partial L}{\partial \dot{q}_i}\right) - \frac{\partial L}{\partial q_j} = Q_j{}^{nc}$$

$L = T - V$

Example 5: A mass M slides down a frictionless plane inclined at angle α. A pendulum, with length l, and mass m, is attached to M. Find the equations of motion. For small oscillation

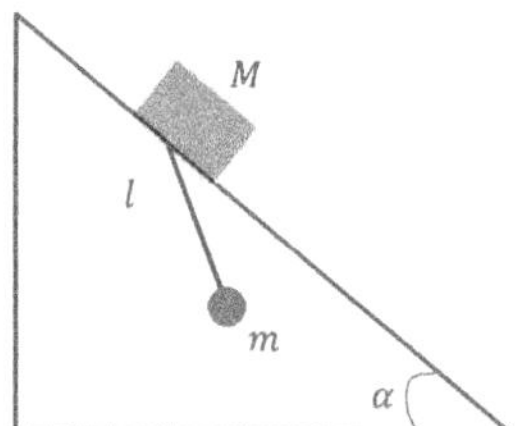

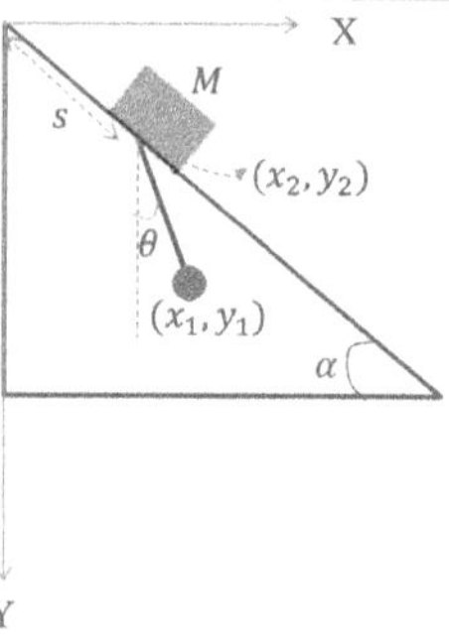

Four constrains equations
$$z_1 = 0; \ z_2 = 0$$
$$y_2 = x_2 \tan \alpha$$
$$(y_2 - y_1)^2 + (x_2 - x_1)^2 = l^2$$

Step-1: *Find the degrees of freedom and choose suitable generalized coordinates*

Two particles $N = 2$, *no. of constrains* $(k) = 4$
      thus degrees of freedom $= 3 \times 2 - 4 = 2$
Hence number of generalized coordinates must be two.

's' and 'θ' can serve as generalized coordinates (they are independent nature)

Step-2: *Find out transformation relations*

$$x_2 = s\,\cos\alpha;\; y_2 = s\,\sin\alpha$$
$$x_1 = s\,\cos\alpha + l\sin\theta\;;\; y_1 = s\,\sin\alpha + l\cos\theta$$

> All the constrains relations have been included in the problem through these relationship

Step-3: *Write T and V in Cartesian*

$$T = \frac{1}{2}m\left(\dot{x}_1{}^2 + \dot{y}_1{}^2\right) + \frac{1}{2}M\left(\dot{x}_2{}^2 + \dot{y}_2{}^2\right)$$
$$\mathrm{V} = -mgy_1 - Mgy_2$$

Step-4:Convert
T and V in generalized coordinate using transformation

$$T = \frac{1}{2}m[\dot{s}^2 + l^2\dot{\theta}^2 + 2l\dot{s}\dot{\theta}\cos(\alpha + \theta)] + \frac{1}{2}M\dot{s}^2$$
$$\mathrm{V} = -mg(s\sin\alpha + l\cos\theta) - Mgs\,\sin\alpha$$

From transformation equation

$$\dot{x}_2 = \dot{s}\,\cos\alpha\;;\; \dot{y}_2 = \dot{s}\sin\alpha$$
$$\dot{x}_1 = \dot{s}\,\cos\alpha + l\cos\theta\,\dot{\theta};$$
$$\dot{y}_1 = \dot{s}\,\sin\alpha - l\sin\theta\,\dot{\theta}$$

Step-5: *Write down Lagrangian*

$$L = T - V$$
$$L = \frac{1}{2}m[\dot{s}^2 + l^2\dot{\theta}^2 + 2l\dot{s}\dot{\theta}\cos(\alpha + \theta)] + \frac{1}{2}M\dot{s}^2$$
$$+mg(s\sin\alpha + l\cos\theta) + Mgs\,\sin\alpha$$

Step-5: *Write down Lagrange's equation for each generalized coordinates*

$$\frac{d}{dt}\left(\frac{\partial L}{\partial \dot{s}}\right) - \frac{\partial L}{\partial s} = 0 \; and \; \frac{d}{dt}\left(\frac{\partial L}{\partial \dot{\theta}}\right) - \frac{\partial L}{\partial \theta} = 0$$

From 1ˢᵗ eqn

$$\frac{d}{dt}[m\dot{s} + ml\dot{\theta}\cos(\alpha + \theta) + M\dot{s}] - mg\sin\alpha - Mg\sin\alpha = 0$$
$$(m + M)\ddot{s} + ml\ddot{\theta}\cos(\alpha + \theta) + ml\dot{\theta}^2\sin(\alpha + \theta) - (m + M)g\sin\alpha = 0$$

From 2ⁿᵈ eqn

$$\frac{d}{dt}[ml^2\dot{\theta} + ml\dot{s}\cos(\alpha + \theta)] + ml\dot{s}\dot{\theta}\sin(\alpha + \theta) + mgl\sin\theta = 0$$
$$ml^2\ddot{\theta} + ml\ddot{s}\cos(\alpha + \theta) + mgl\sin\theta = 0$$

Problems with generalized force

Example-6

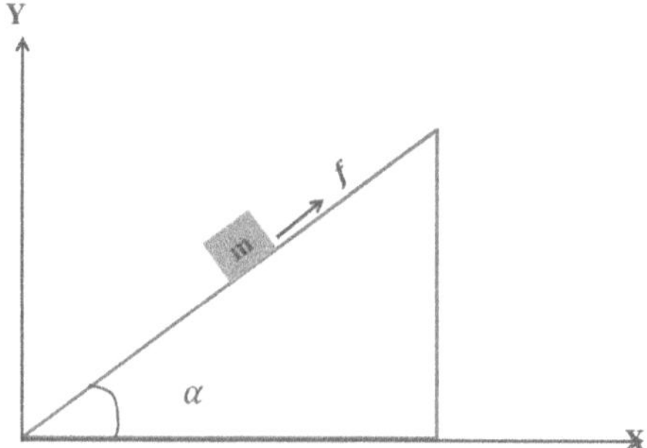

Find $\theta(t)$?

$$f = C\dot{\theta}^2$$

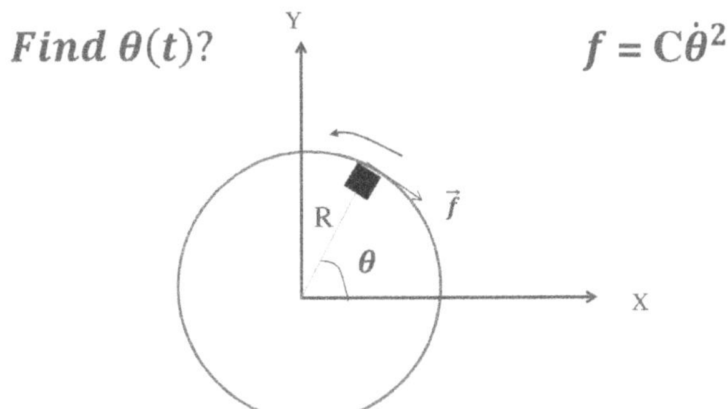

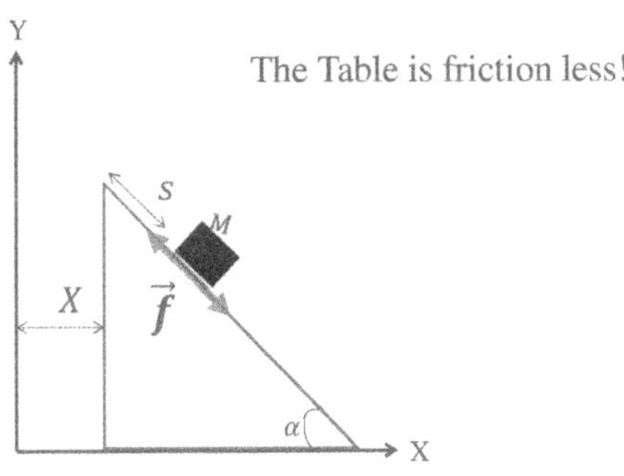

Generalized coordinate (X, s)

History of Variational Calculus (Wikipedia/Rana&Joag)

Pierre de Fermat
(1607 –1665)

Isaac Newton
(1642 – 1727)

Jacob Bernoulli
(1655 – 1705)
Algebra

Johann (Jean or John)
Bernoulli (1667 –1748)
Variational calculus

Leonhard Euler
(1707-1783)

Joseph-Louis
Lagrange

Daniel Bernoulli (1700 –1782)
Bernoulli's principle on fluids

Fermat's principle of least (extremum) time ~1662

$$n = \frac{\text{speed of light in vacuum}}{\text{speed of light in medium}}$$

(n=1.33)

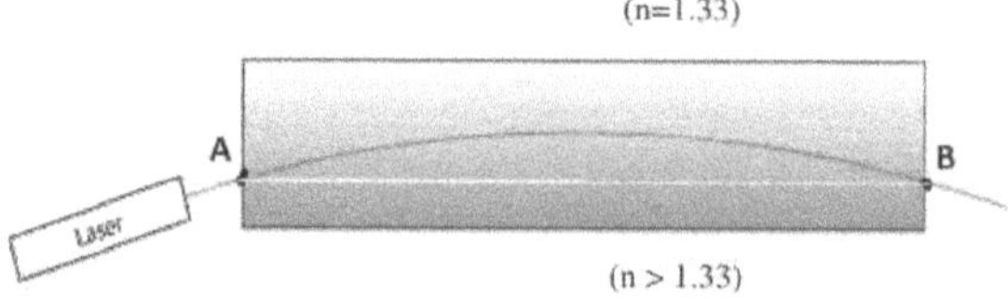

www.physicsforums.com

Page 67 of 94,Mechanics: An Easy Approach by Bikash Kumar Naik

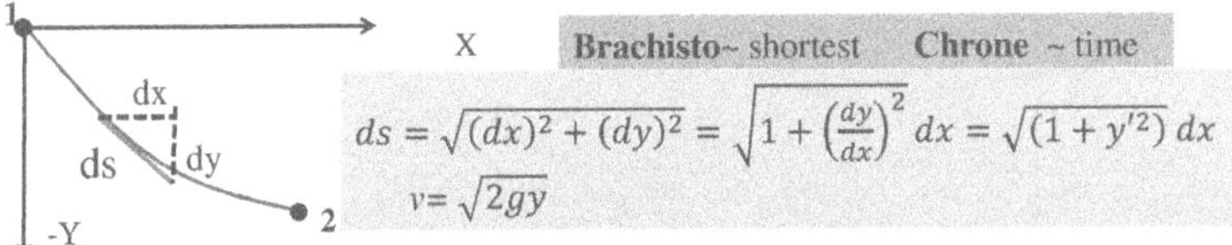

Jean Bernoulli's challenge!
"Brachistochrone"

❑ What should be the shape of a stone's trajectory (or, of a roller coaster track) so that released from point 1 it reaches point 2 in the shortest possible time? **Brachistochrone problem!**   ~1696

X   **Brachisto~** shortest   **Chrone** ~ time

$$ds = \sqrt{(dx)^2 + (dy)^2} = \sqrt{1 + \left(\frac{dy}{dx}\right)^2}\, dx = \sqrt{(1 + y'^2)}\, dx$$

$$v = \sqrt{2gy}$$

❑ Time (from 1 to 2) $I = \int_1^2 \frac{ds}{v} = \int_1^2 \frac{\sqrt{(1+y'^2)}}{\sqrt{2gy}}\, dx = \int_1^2 F(y, y', x)\, dx$

Cycloid

Wiki

Extremums!

Can we prove mathematically
❑ Shortest distance between two points is a straight line?

❑ Shortest path between two points on the surface of a sphere is along the **great-circle**?

❑ To answer these questions, one need to know necessary condition that the integral $I = \int_{x_1}^{x_2} F(y, y', x)\, dx$, where $y = y(x), y' = \frac{dy}{dx}$

is **stationary**

(**ie, an extremum!** – either a maximum or a minimum!).

❑ **Interestingly we are already familiar with the solution!**

Extremum of a function

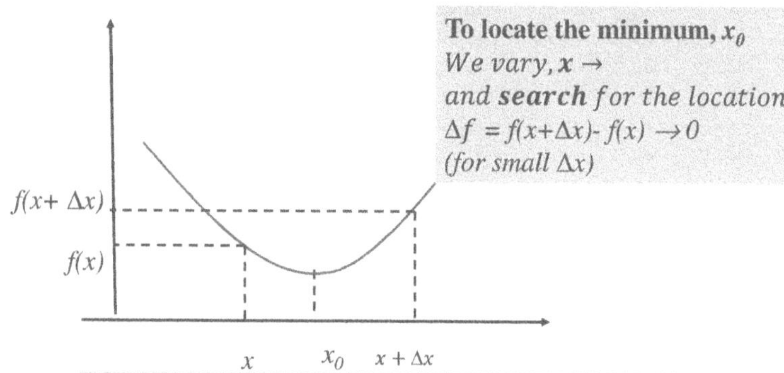

To locate the minimum, x_0
We vary, $x \rightarrow$
and **search** *for the location*
$\Delta f = f(x+\Delta x) - f(x) \rightarrow 0$
(for small Δx)

$f(x+\Delta x)$

$f(x)$

$x \qquad x_0 \qquad x+\Delta x$

We say the function is **stationary** at, x_0
(Meaning, for small steps, Δx, at x_0 the value of the
function does not change. $\Delta f = \left(\dfrac{\partial f}{\partial x}\right)_{x0} \Delta x = 0$

Possible integration paths

❑ Out of the **infinite** number of **possible paths,** $y(x)$,
which path makes the integral,

$$I = \int_{x_1}^{x_2} F(y, y', x)\, dx \qquad \text{-stationary?}$$

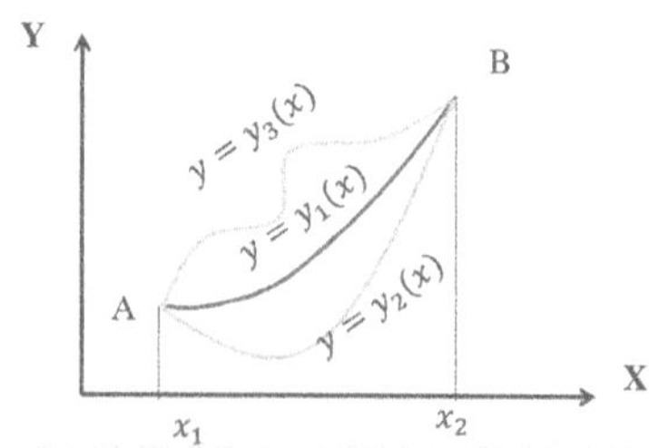

We need to find the condition for an
integral to be stationary, where the **variable is a "function"**
itself $[y = y(x)]$ -the integration path!

Smart choice of varied paths

- ❏ **Step 1:** Let's assume $y(x) = Y(x)$ as the path for which integral,
$$I = \int_{x_1}^{x_2} F(y, \dot{y}, x)\, dx \quad \text{is } \textbf{stationary.}$$

- ❏ **Step2:** $y(x) = Y(x) + \Delta y(x)$ can represent all possible paths between x_1 and x_2 for different $\Delta y(x)$.

Can you choose suitable mathematical form of $\Delta y(x)$ such that

(i) $y(x) = Y(x) + \Delta y(x)$ should represent all varied paths but must not have variations at $A(x_1)$ and $B(x_2)$ (fixed points).

(ii) $\Delta y(x)$ goes to zero in the limiting case when the varied paths are very close to $Y(x)$.

Let's check this choice $\Delta y(x) = \epsilon\, \eta(x)$

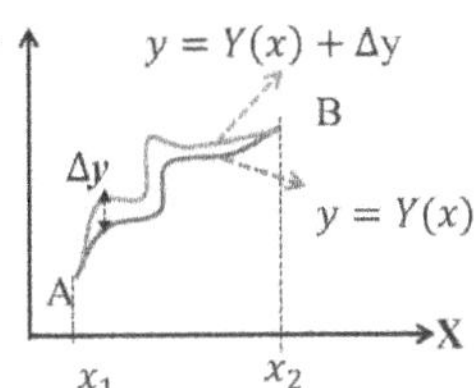

- ➤ where $\eta(x)$ is any **arbitrary function** of x such that $\eta(x_1) = \eta(x_2) = 0$. [condition (i) satisfied]

- ➤ ϵ is a parameter which can vary from 0 to higher value continuously. If we take **limit $\epsilon \to 0$**, then condition (ii) satisfied.

$\eta(x)$ and ϵ are indeed smart choice

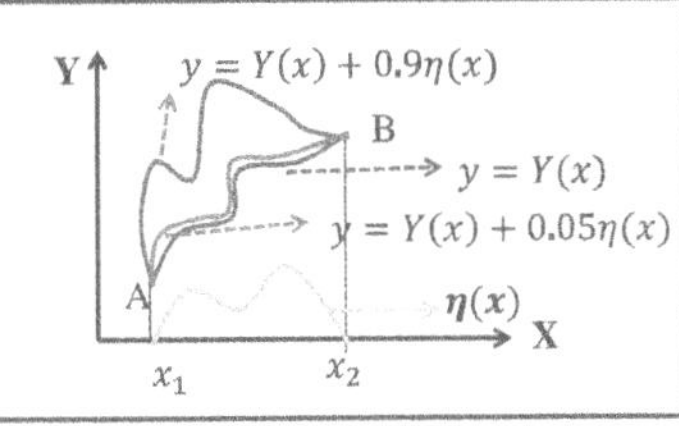

Typical choice of arbitrary function $\eta(x)$,

- ➤ $\eta(x_1) = \eta(x_2) = 0$.
- ➤ By varying ϵ, different strength of $\eta(x)$ can be added to $Y(x)$ to generate range of possible paths between A and B.
- ➤ $\epsilon \to 0$ gives us the true path $Y(x)$.

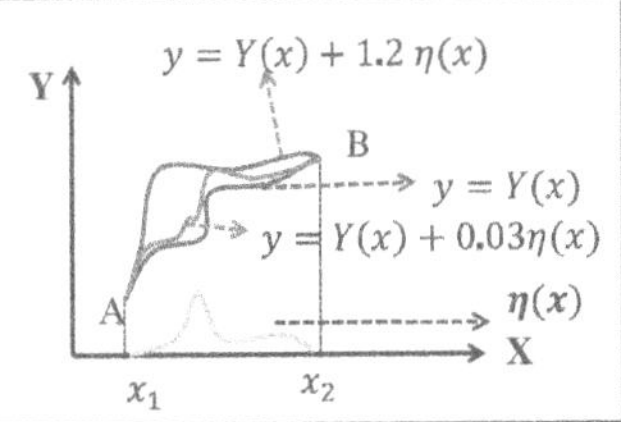

For another choice of $\eta(x)$ to generate another series of possible paths between A and B by varying ϵ.

Thus arbitrary $\eta(x)$ and ϵ can produce all possible paths.

Step 3: Variation of the integral value for different paths nearby to the stationary path $Y(x)$ [ie, $\epsilon \to 0$ *hence* $\Delta y \to 0$], is negligibly small.

The meaning of the statement is

Integration $I = \int_{x_1}^{x_2} F(Y, Y', x)dx$ along stationary path $y(x) = Y(x)$

and

integration along the **nearby paths** $[y(x, \epsilon) = Y + \Delta y = Y(x) + \epsilon\eta(x)$, *and* $\epsilon \to 0$]

$$I(\epsilon) = \int_{x_1}^{x_2} F\{(Y + \Delta y), (Y' + \Delta y'), x\}dx] = \int_{x_1}^{x_2} F\{y(x, \epsilon), y'(x, \epsilon), x\}dx$$

must be equal. i.e, $\delta I(\epsilon) = 0, \epsilon \to 0$

This can be achieved by, $\left.\dfrac{dI(\epsilon)}{d\epsilon}\right|_{\epsilon \to 0} = 0$

For stationary path $\left.\dfrac{dI(\epsilon)}{d\epsilon}\right|_{\epsilon \to 0} = \mathbf{0}$

$$\left.\frac{dI(\epsilon)}{d\epsilon}\right|_{\epsilon \to 0} = \frac{d}{d\epsilon}\left[\int_{x_1}^{x_2} F\{y(x, \epsilon), y'(x, \epsilon), x\}dx\right]$$

Where,
$$y(x, \epsilon) = (Y + \epsilon\eta)$$
$$y'(x, \epsilon) = Y' + \epsilon\eta'$$

$$= \int_{x_1}^{x_2}\left(\frac{\partial F}{\partial y}\frac{\partial y}{\partial \epsilon} + \frac{\partial F}{\partial y'}\frac{\partial y'}{\partial \epsilon}\right)dx = \int_{x_1}^{x_2}\frac{\partial F}{\partial y}\eta\, dx + \int_{x_1}^{x_2}\frac{\partial F}{\partial y'}\eta'dx$$

$$= \int_{x_1}^{x_2}\frac{\partial F}{\partial y}\eta\, dx + \left.\frac{\partial F}{\partial y'}\eta\right|_{x_1}^{x_2} - \int_{x_1}^{x_2}\frac{d}{dx}\left(\frac{\partial F}{\partial y'}\right)\eta dx \quad \Longleftarrow \text{ Integration by parts}$$

$$\mathbf{Using}\ \left.\frac{\partial F}{\partial y'}\eta\right|_{x_1}^{x_2} = 0$$

As $\eta(x_1) = \eta(x_2) = 0$

$$= -\int_{x_1}^{x_2}\left[\frac{d}{dx}\left(\frac{\partial F}{\partial y'}\right) - \frac{\partial F}{\partial y}\right]\eta\, dx = 0$$

This equation is true for any possible choice of $\eta(x)$, thus

$$\frac{d}{dx}\left(\frac{\partial F}{\partial y'}\right) - \frac{\partial F}{\partial y} = 0,$$

Euler-Lagrange equation!

This is necessary condition for $I = \int_{x_1}^{x_2} F(y, \dot{y}, x)dx$ to be stationary!

❑ Given two points in a plane, what is the shortest path between them? We certainly know the answer: Straight line. Let's prove it using variation method

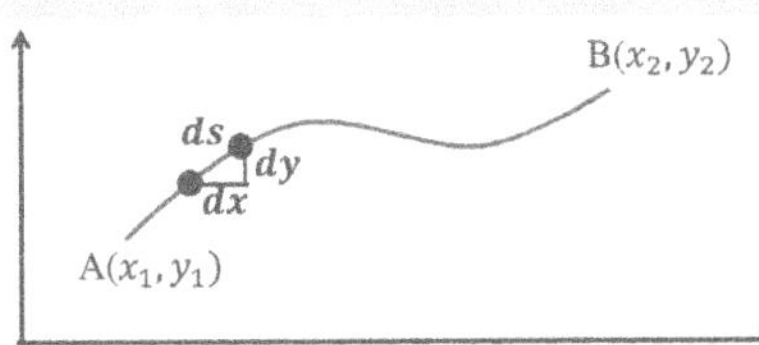

❑ Consider an arbitrary path $y(x)$, elementary length

❑ $ds = \sqrt{(dx)^2 + (dy)^2} = \left[\left\{1 + \left(\frac{dy}{dx}\right)^2\right\}\right]^{1/2} dx = \sqrt{(1 + y'^2)}\, dx$

❑ Total path length $\int_A^B ds = \int_{x_1}^{x_2} \sqrt{(1 + y'^2)}\, dx$

❑ Necessary condition for this integral to be stationary (maximum)

$\frac{d}{dx}\left(\frac{\partial F}{\partial y'}\right) - \frac{\partial F}{\partial y} = 0$; Here $F(y, y', x) = (1 + y'^2)^{1/2}$

Application of variational principle: Example1

$$\frac{\partial F}{\partial y'} = \frac{\partial}{\partial y'}\left\{\sqrt{(1 + y'^2)}\right\} = \frac{y'}{\sqrt{(1 + y'^2)}}$$

$$\frac{\partial F}{\partial y} = 0 \rightarrow \frac{y'}{\sqrt{(1 + y'^2)}} = A \quad \text{const.}$$

Thus

$$y'^2 = A^2(1 + y'^2)$$
$$y'^2(1 - A^2) = A^2$$
$$y' = \sqrt{\frac{A^2}{(1 - A^2)}} = m$$
$$y(x) = mx + C,$$
$$\textit{Where m and C are constant}$$

Equation of straight line.

❑ Shortest distance between two points in a plane is straight line.

❑ What should be the tailored trajectory of a mass, m, which when released from point 1 will reach point 2 in the shortest possible time? **Brachistochrone problem**

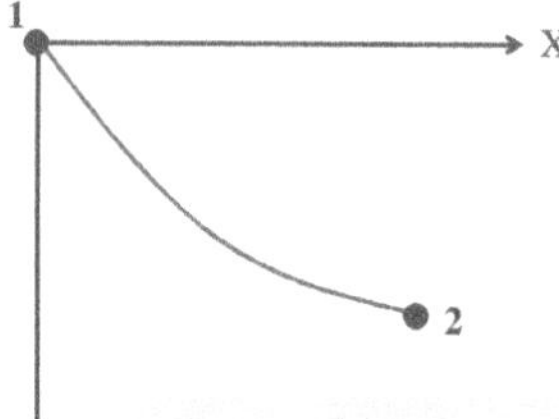

❑ Time to travel from 1 to 2

Time $(1 \rightarrow 2) = \int_1^2 \frac{ds}{v}$

$ds \rightarrow Elementary\ path\ length$
$v \rightarrow Instantaneous\ velocity$

❑ From energy conservation, $\frac{1}{2}mv^2 = mgy\ ; v = (2gy)^{1/2}$

$$ds = [(dx)^2 + (dy)^2]^{1/2} = \left[\left\{1 + \left(\frac{dx}{dy}\right)^2\right\}\right]^{1/2} dy = \left(1 + x'^2\right)^{1/2} dy \qquad x' = \frac{dx}{dy}$$

❑ Time to travel from 1 to 2

Time1 $\rightarrow$ 2)

$$= \int_1^2 \frac{ds}{v} = \int_0^{y_2} \frac{\left(1 + x'^2\right)^{1/2}}{(2gy)^{1/2}} dy = \int_0^{y_2} F\{x(y), x'(y), y\} dy$$

What about $F\{y(x), y'(x), x\}$?
Then $\frac{\partial F}{\partial y} \neq 0$
Mathematically harder!

Where,

$$F\{x(y), x'(y), y\} = \frac{\left(1 + x'^2\right)^{1/2}}{(2gy)^{1/2}}$$

❑ Necessary condition for the integral (total time) to be extremum

$$\frac{d}{dy}\left(\frac{\partial F}{\partial x'}\right) - \frac{\partial F}{\partial x} = 0$$

$$\frac{\partial F}{\partial x'} = \frac{\partial}{\partial x'}\left\{\frac{\left(1+x'^2\right)^{1/2}}{(2gy)^{1/2}}\right\} = \frac{x'\left(1+x'^2\right)^{-1/2}}{(2gy)^{1/2}}; \qquad \frac{\partial F}{\partial x} = 0$$

$$\frac{d}{dy}\left[\frac{x'\left(1+x'^2\right)^{-1/2}}{(2gy)^{1/2}}\right] = 0; \text{ Hence } \frac{x'\left(1+x'^2\right)^{-1/2}}{(2gy)^{1/2}} = Constant;$$

$$\frac{x'^2}{y\left(1+x'^2\right)} = Constant = \frac{1}{2a}$$

❑ To solve the integral, substitute $y = a(1 - \cos\theta) \dots\dots(1)$

$$\text{thus } dy = a\sin\theta\, d\theta$$

$$x = \int \sqrt{\frac{a(1-\cos\theta)}{a(1+\cos\theta)}}\, a\sin\theta\, d\theta = a\int \sqrt{\frac{(1-\cos\theta)}{(1+\cos\theta)}}\sqrt{(1-\cos\theta)(1+\cos\theta)}\, d\theta$$

$$x = a\int(1-\cos\theta)\, d\theta; \qquad x = a(\theta - \sin\theta) + constant\dots(2)$$

❑ $L(q_j, \dot{q}_j, t) \rightarrow$ Lagrangian of system of particles

❑ **Action integral** $\longrightarrow \displaystyle\int_{t_1}^{t_2} L(q_j, \dot{q}_j, t)\, dt$

❑ A mechanical system will evolve in time in such that action integral is stationary $\rightarrow$ **Hamilton's Principle of Least Action**

$$\int_{t_1}^{t_2} L(q_j, \dot{q}_j, t)\, dt \longrightarrow \textbf{Stationary} \longrightarrow \delta\int_{t_1}^{t_2} L(q_j, \dot{q}_j, t)\, dt = 0$$

❑ Stationary condition of Action integral

$$\frac{d}{dt}\left(\frac{\partial L}{\partial \dot{q}_j}\right) - \frac{\partial L}{\partial q_j} = 0 \longrightarrow$$ ❑ Lagrange's equation from Variational principle

symmetries and conservation laws

Cyclic coordinates, symmetries and conservation laws

Cyclic coordinate (q_j)  Corresponding generalized (canonical) momentum $(p_j = \frac{\partial L}{\partial \dot{q}_j})$ conserved

L is independent of the particular cyclic coordinate (q_j).
$q_j \rightarrow q_j + \delta q_j$ has no effect on L.

System is symmetric under **translation in generalized coordinate** q_j

❑ **Symmetry in generalized coordinate gives rise to a conserved canonical momentum.**

Example: For planetary motion

$$L = \frac{1}{2}m\left(\dot{r}^2 + r^2\dot{\theta}^2\right) + \frac{GMm}{r}$$

L is independent of rotation angle θ(cyclic coordinate), the system has rotational symmetry [symmetric under translation in $\theta \rightarrow \theta + \delta\theta$) , the system remains the same after change in θ.

As θ is cyclic, corresponding generalized (canonical) momentum $p_\theta = mr^2\dot{\theta}$=Constant; which is nothing but angular momentum.

Conclusion: Conservation of angular momentum is related to rotational symmetry of the system.

Translational symmetry and homogeneity of space

❑ **Homogeneity of space**: Space is such that in a particular direction, all the points are equivalent.

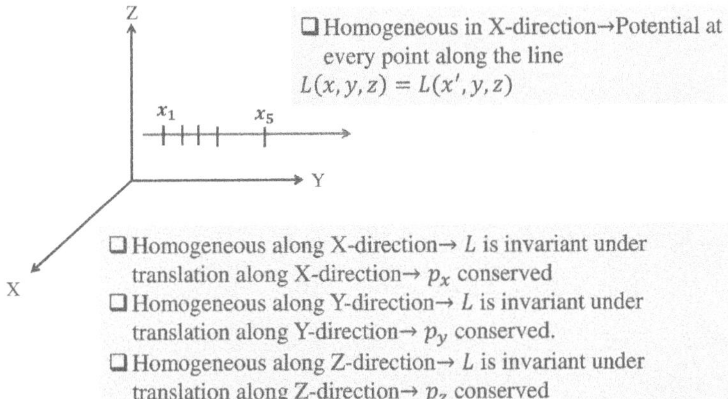

❑ Homogeneous in X-direction→Potential at every point along the line
$$L(x, y, z) = L(x', y, z)$$

❑ Homogeneous along X-direction→ L is invariant under translation along X-direction→ p_x conserved
❑ Homogeneous along Y-direction→ L is invariant under translation along Y-direction→ p_y conserved.
❑ Homogeneous along Z-direction→ L is invariant under translation along Z-direction→ p_z conserved

Rotational symmetry and isotropy of space

❑ **Isotropy of space**: Different directions around a point are all equivalent (at the same distance from that point).

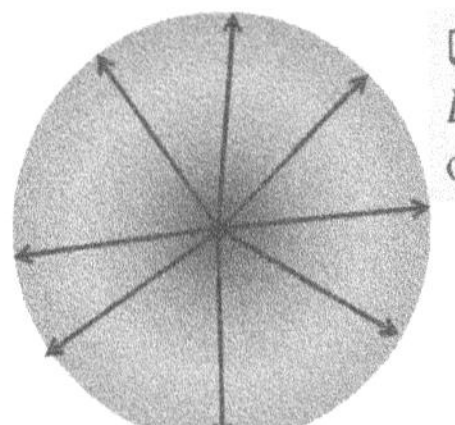

❑ Thus→
$L(r, \theta, \varphi, \psi) = L(r, \theta', \varphi', \psi)$, function of r only.

Isotropy of space≡ Rotational symmetry of the system in both θ, φ and ψ

❑ All the directions are equivalent
❑ Potential energy in different directions (at the same distance from a particular point) must be same, as all directions are equivalent.
❑ Thus $L(r)$, *independent of* θ, φ and ψ. , L is invariant under rotation.
❑ p_φ and p_θ and p_ψ are conserved.

Symmetry and conservation laws

Homogeneity of space (Translational symmetry)	$\Rightarrow$ Conservation of linear momentum
Isotropy of space (Rotational symmetry)	$\Rightarrow$ Conservation of angular momentum

Homogeneity in time?

$$L(q_j, \dot{q}_j, t) = L(q_j, \dot{q}_j, t')$$

Only possible if L does not have explicit time dependence

Homogeneity in time ("translation" in time)	$\Rightarrow$ Conservation of energy

❑ If L does not explicitly depend on time, then energy of the system is conserved, provided potential energy is velocity independent.

Homogeneity in time leads to energy conservation: Proof

❑ $L = L(q_1, \ldots q_n, \dot{q}_1, \ldots \dot{q}_n, t)$

❑ Using the chain rule of partial differentiation

$$\frac{dL}{dt} = \sum_j \frac{\partial L}{\partial \dot{q}_j} \ddot{q}_j + \sum_j \frac{\partial L}{\partial q_j} \dot{q}_j + \frac{\partial L}{\partial t}$$

$$\frac{dL}{dt} = \sum_j \frac{\partial L}{\partial \dot{q}_j} \ddot{q}_j + \sum_j \frac{d}{dt}\left(\frac{\partial L}{\partial \dot{q}_j}\right) \dot{q}_j + \frac{\partial L}{\partial t}$$

❑ Using Lagrange's eqn.

$$\frac{d}{dt}\left(\frac{\partial L}{\partial \dot{q}_j}\right) - \frac{\partial L}{\partial q_j} = 0$$

$$\frac{dL}{dt} = \sum_j \frac{d}{dt}\left(\frac{\partial L}{\partial \dot{q}_j}\dot{q}_j\right) + \frac{\partial L}{\partial t}$$

$$\frac{d}{dt}\left(\sum_j \frac{\partial L}{\partial \dot{q}_j}\dot{q}_j - L\right) + \frac{\partial L}{\partial t} = 0 \quad \text{----------------- [1]}$$

❑ If L does not have explicit time dependence

$$i, e \ \frac{\partial L}{\partial t} = 0$$

 $$\sum_j \frac{\partial L}{\partial \dot{q}_j}\dot{q}_j - L = Constant \quad \text{----------} \boxed{2}$$

$$\sum_j \frac{\partial L}{\partial \dot{q}_j} \dot{q}_j = 2T$$

- ❑ If V does not depend on generalized velocity, $\frac{\partial V}{\partial \dot{q}_j} = 0$; $\frac{\partial L}{\partial \dot{q}_j} = \frac{\partial T}{\partial \dot{q}_j}$ as $L = T - V$

- ❑ If L does not explicitly depend on time $(\frac{\partial L}{\partial t} = 0)$ and V is velocity independent,
$$\sum_j \frac{\partial T}{\partial \dot{q}_j} \dot{q}_j - L = Constant$$

- ❑ For a single free particle $T = \frac{1}{2} m(\dot{x}^2 + \dot{y}^2 + \dot{z}^2)$
$$\sum_j \frac{\partial T}{\partial \dot{q}_j} \dot{q}_j = m(\dot{x}\dot{x} + \dot{y}\dot{y} + \dot{z}\dot{z}) = 2T$$

- ❑ The relationship is true for General case as well,

Euler's theorem: If $f(x_i)$ is a homogeneous function of the n_{th} degree of set of variables x_i, then $\sum_j \frac{\partial f}{\partial x_j} \dot{x}_j = nf.$

- ❑ Kinetic energy T is a function of 2nd degree of generalized velocities $\dot{q}_j$

Proof continue…

$$\sum_j \frac{\partial T}{\partial \dot{q}_j} \dot{q}_j - L = Constant$$

Now, $$\sum_j \frac{\partial T}{\partial \dot{q}_j} \dot{q}_j = 2T$$

$$(2T - L) = constant$$
$$(2T - T + V) = constant$$
$$T + V = constant$$

Conclusion, $T + V = E = constant$,
*if L does not explicitely depend on time
and potential is velocity indepdent*

- ❑ Total energy conserved if

L does not depend not explicitly depend on time→Change in time does not cause any change in the form of L →Homogeneity in time

❑ **Principle of least action:** Action I= $\int_{t_1}^{t_2} L(q_j, \dot{q}_j, t)dt$ is stationary

$$\frac{d}{dt}\left(\frac{\partial L}{\partial \dot{q}_j}\right) - \frac{\partial L}{\partial q_j} = 0$$

❑ If L does not have explicit time dependence, i,e $L = L(q_1, \dots q_n, \dot{q}_1, \dots \dot{q}_n)$

$$\sum_j \frac{\partial L}{\partial \dot{q}_j}\dot{q}_j - L = Constant$$

❑ $I = \int_{x_1}^{x_2} F(x, y, y')dx$ stationary $\Rightarrow \frac{d}{dx}\left(\frac{\partial F}{\partial y'}\right) - \frac{\partial F}{\partial y} = 0$

If F does not have explicit dependence on x, i,e $F = F(y, y')$

$$\frac{\partial F}{\partial y'}y' - F = Constant$$

Homogeneity in space	Conservation of linear momentum
Isotropy of space	Conservation of angular momentum
Homogeneity in time	Conservation of energy

Application of variation principle: Shortest path between two points on the surface of a sphere

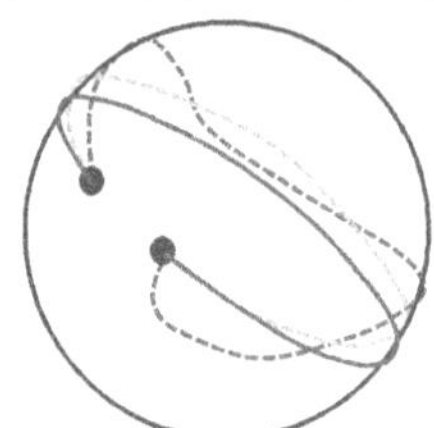

❑ Shortest path is the path along the great circle connecting the two points

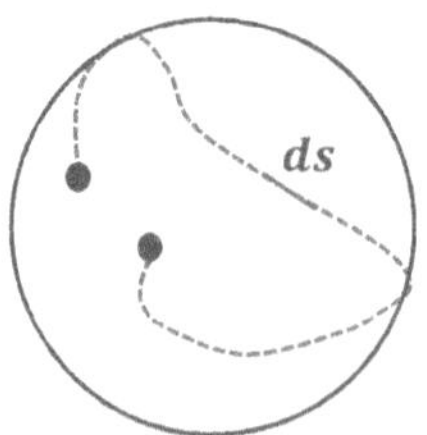

❑ Elementary length (ds) between two points in spherical polar coordinates

$$ds^2 = dr^2 + r^2 d\theta^2 + r^2 sin^2\theta \, d\varphi^2$$

❑ On the surface of the sphere,
$$r = R = constant$$
$$\dot{r} = 0$$
$$ds^2 = R^2 d\theta^2 + R^2 sin^2\theta \, d\varphi^2$$

Shortest path between two points on the surface of a sphere

☐ Total length between two points 1&2

$$S = \int_1^2 ds = \int_1^2 \sqrt{R^2 d\theta^2 + R^2 \sin^2\theta \, d\varphi^2}$$

$$S = R\int_{\theta_1}^{\theta_2} \sqrt{1 + \sin^2\theta \left(\frac{d\varphi}{d\theta}\right)^2} \, d\theta$$

Mathematically difficult due to non-zero $\frac{\partial F}{\partial \theta}$

☐ You can also express as

$$S = R\int_{\varphi_1}^{\varphi_2} \sqrt{\sin^2\theta + \left(\frac{d\theta}{d\varphi}\right)^2} \, d\varphi$$

$$F\{\theta, \varphi(\theta), \varphi'(\theta)\} = \sqrt{1 + \sin^2\theta \left(\frac{d\varphi}{d\theta}\right)^2} = \sqrt{1 + \sin^2\theta \varphi'^2} \qquad \varphi' = \frac{d\varphi}{d\theta}$$

☐ Necessary condition for the integral (total time) to be extremum

$$\frac{d}{d\theta}\left(\frac{\partial F}{\partial \varphi'}\right) - \frac{\partial F}{\partial \varphi} = 0$$

Shortest path between two points on the surface of a sphere

$$F = \sqrt{1 + \sin^2\theta \, \varphi'^2} \qquad \frac{\partial F}{\partial \varphi} = 0 \qquad \frac{\partial F}{\partial \varphi'} = \frac{\sin^2\theta \varphi'}{\sqrt{1 + \sin^2\theta \, \varphi'^2}}$$

$$\frac{d}{d\theta}\left(\frac{\sin^2\theta \varphi'}{\sqrt{1 + \sin^2\theta \, \varphi'^2}}\right) = 0; \qquad \frac{\sin^2\theta \varphi'}{\sqrt{1 + \sin^2\theta \, \varphi'^2}} = constant = k$$

$$\sin^4\theta\varphi'^2 = k^2\left(1 + \sin^2\theta \, \varphi'^2\right); \qquad \varphi' = \pm\frac{k \csc^2\theta}{\sqrt{1 - k^2\csc^2\theta}}$$

$$\varphi' = \pm\frac{k \csc^2\theta}{\sqrt{1 - k^2(1 + \cot^2\theta)}} = \pm\frac{k \csc^2\theta}{\sqrt{1 - k^2 - k^2\cot^2\theta}}$$

$$\varphi' = \frac{\pm k}{\sqrt{1 - k^2}}\frac{\csc^2\theta}{\sqrt{1 - \frac{k^2}{1 - k^2}\cot^2\theta}}$$

$$d\varphi = \alpha \frac{\csc^2\theta \, d\theta}{\sqrt{1 - \alpha^2 \cot^2\theta}}$$

$$d\varphi = \frac{dq}{\sqrt{1-q^2}} \; ; \int d\varphi = \int \frac{dq}{\sqrt{1-q^2}}$$

$$\varphi = \sin^{-1} q + \beta; q = \sin(\varphi - \beta)$$

$$\boldsymbol{\alpha \cot\theta = \sin(\varphi - \beta)} \ldots \ldots [1]$$

Let $\alpha = \frac{\pm k}{\sqrt{1-k^2}}$ and $q = \alpha \cot\theta$

$$dq = \alpha \csc^2\theta \, d\theta$$

$\beta \rightarrow Integration \; constant$

To understand the meaning of **equation 1**, multiply both sides by R

$$\alpha R \cot\theta = R \sin(\varphi - \beta)$$
$$\alpha R \cos\theta = R \sin\theta \sin\varphi \cos\beta - R \sin\theta \cos\varphi \sin\beta$$
$$\alpha z = \cos\beta \, y - \sin\beta \, x$$
$$\boldsymbol{\sin\beta \, x - \cos\beta \, y - \alpha z = 0}$$

$\longrightarrow$ Equation of a plane passing through origin

Equation of a plane passing through (x_0, y_0, z_0)
$$a(x - x_0) + b(y - y_0) + c(z - z_0) = 0$$

$$\sin\beta \, x - \cos\beta \, y - \alpha z = 0$$

This plane which passes through the origin slices through the sphere in great circles

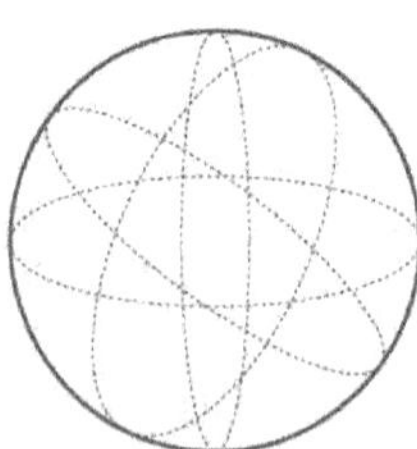

Thus solution of Euler-Lagrange's equation are great circle routes

Shortest path between two points on the surface of a sphere must lie on this the great circle passing through those points.

- $L = L(q_1, \dots q_n, \dot{q}_1, \dots \dot{q}_n, t)$
- Using the chain rule of partial differentiation

$$\frac{dL}{dt} = \sum_j \frac{\partial L}{\partial \dot{q}_j} \ddot{q}_j + \sum_j \frac{\partial L}{\partial q_j} \dot{q}_j + \frac{\partial L}{\partial t}$$

$$\frac{dL}{dt} = \sum_j \frac{\partial L}{\partial \dot{q}_j} \ddot{q}_j + \sum_j \frac{d}{dt}\left(\frac{\partial L}{\partial \dot{q}_j}\right) \dot{q}_j + \frac{\partial L}{\partial t}$$

- Using Lagrange's eqn.

$$\frac{d}{dt}\left(\frac{\partial L}{\partial \dot{q}_j}\right) - \frac{\partial L}{\partial q_j} = 0$$

$$\frac{dL}{dt} = \sum_j \frac{d}{dt}\left(\frac{\partial L}{\partial \dot{q}_j}\dot{q}_j\right) + \frac{\partial L}{\partial t}$$

$$\frac{d}{dt}\left(\sum_j \frac{\partial L}{\partial \dot{q}_j}\dot{q}_j - L\right) + \frac{\partial L}{\partial t} = 0$$

$$\frac{d}{dt}\left(\sum_j p_j \dot{q}_j - L\right) + \frac{\partial L}{\partial t} = 0$$

$$p_j = \frac{\partial L}{\partial \dot{q}_j}$$

Hamiltonian $H(q_j, \dot{q}_j, t)$

$$\frac{d}{dt}\left(\sum_j p_j \dot{q}_j - L\right) + \frac{\partial L}{\partial t} = 0$$

- Can introduce new function

$$h(q_j, p_j, \dot{q}_j, t) = \sum_j p_j \dot{q}_j - L(q_j, \dot{q}_j, t)$$

- If $\dot{q}_j$ is substituted with p_j using their relation obtained from $p_j = \frac{\partial L}{\partial \dot{q}_j}$, then the function is known as **Hamiltonian**

$$H(q_j, p_j, t) = \sum_j p_j \dot{q}_j - L$$

$h(q_j, p_j, \dot{q}_j, t)$ — Substitute $\dot{q}_j$ with p_j → $H(q_j, p_j, t)$

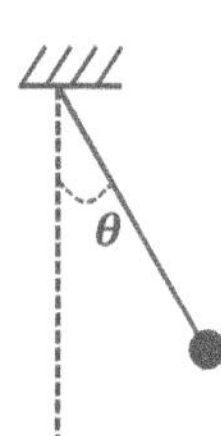

Step 1: Find Lagrangian of the system

$$L = \frac{1}{2}ml^2\dot{\theta}^2 + mgl\,cos\theta$$

Step 2: Find generalized momentum (p_j) using $p_j = \frac{\partial L}{\partial \dot{q}_j}$

$$p_\theta = \frac{\partial L}{\partial \dot{\theta}} == \frac{\partial}{\partial \dot{\theta}}\left(\frac{1}{2}ml^2\dot{\theta}^2 + mgl\,cos\theta\right) = ml^2\dot{\theta}$$

Step 3: Find the function $h\left(q_j, p_j, \dot{q}_j, t\right) = \sum p_j\dot{q}_j - L$

$$h = p_\theta\dot{\theta} - \frac{1}{2}ml^2\dot{\theta}^2 - mgl\,cos\theta$$

Step 4: Find Hamiltonian $H\left(q_j, p_j, t\right)$ from h by replacing $\dot{q}_j$ with p_j using step-2

$$H(q_j, p_j, t) = p_\theta\,\frac{p_\theta}{ml^2} - \frac{1}{2}ml^2\left(\frac{p_\theta}{ml^2}\right)^2 - mgl\,cos\theta = \frac{p_\theta{}^2}{2ml^2} - mgl\,cos\theta$$

Hamiltonian Example 2: Projectile

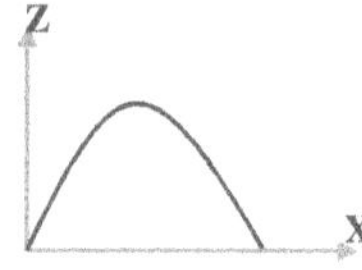

Step 1: Find Lagrangian of the system

$$L = \frac{1}{2}m(\dot{x}^2 + \dot{z}^2) - mgz$$

Step 2: Find generalized momentum (p_j) using $p_j = \frac{\partial L}{\partial \dot{q}_j}$

$$p_x = \frac{\partial L}{\partial \dot{x}} = m\dot{x} \quad ; \quad p_z = \frac{\partial L}{\partial \dot{z}} = m\dot{z}$$

Step 3: Find the function $h\left(q_j, p_j, \dot{q}_j, t\right) = \sum p_j\dot{q}_j - L$

$$h(x, z, \dot{x}, \dot{z}, t) = p_x\dot{x} + p_z\dot{z} - \frac{1}{2}m(\dot{x}^2 + \dot{z}^2) + mgz$$

Step 4: Find Hamiltonian $H\left(q_j, p_j, t\right)$ from h by replacing $\dot{q}_j$ with p_j using step-2

$$H(x, z, p_x, p_z, t) = p_x\frac{p_x}{m} + p_z\frac{p_z}{m} - \frac{1}{2}m\left(\frac{p_x{}^2}{m^2} + \frac{p_z{}^2}{m^2}\right) + mgz$$

$$= \frac{p_x{}^2}{2m} + \frac{p_z{}^2}{2m} + mgz$$

Hamilton's equations

$$H(q_j, p_j, t) = \sum_j p_j \dot{q}_j - L$$

$$dH(q_j, p_j, t) = d\left[\sum_j p_j \dot{q}_j - L\right]$$

$$L.H.S = dH(q_j, p_j, t)$$
$$= \sum_j \frac{\partial H}{\partial q_j} dq_j + \sum_j \frac{\partial H}{\partial p_j} dp_j + \frac{\partial H}{\partial t} dt$$

$$R.H.S = d\left[\sum_j p_j \dot{q}_j - L\right] = d\sum_j p_j \dot{q}_j - dL$$

$$= \sum_j \left(\dot{q}_j dp_j + p_j d\dot{q}_j\right) - \left[\left(\sum_j \frac{\partial L}{\partial q_j} dq_j + \frac{\partial L}{\partial \dot{q}_j} d\dot{q}_j\right) + \frac{\partial L}{\partial t} dt\right]$$

Hamilton's equations

$$dH(q_j, p_j, t) = d\left[\sum_j p_j \dot{q}_j - L\right]$$

$$\sum_j \frac{\partial H}{\partial q_j} dq_j + \sum_j \frac{\partial H}{\partial p_j} dp_j + \frac{\partial H}{\partial t} dt$$

$$= \sum_j \left(\dot{q}_j dp_j + p_j d\dot{q}_j\right) - \sum_j \frac{\partial L}{\partial q_j} dq_j - \sum_j \frac{\partial L}{\partial \dot{q}_j} d\dot{q}_j - \frac{\partial L}{\partial t} dt$$

$$= \sum_j \left(\dot{q}_j dp_j + p_j d\dot{q}_j\right) - \sum_j \dot{p}_j dq_j - \sum_j p_j d\dot{q}_j - \frac{\partial L}{\partial t} dt$$

$$= \sum_j \dot{q}_j dp_j - \sum_j \dot{p}_j dq_j - \frac{\partial L}{\partial t} dt$$

$$\dot{p}_j = -\frac{\partial H}{\partial q_j}; \quad \dot{q}_j = \frac{\partial H}{\partial p_j} \qquad \text{Hamilton's equations} \qquad \frac{\partial H}{\partial t} = -\frac{\partial L}{\partial t}$$

Hamilton's equations $\implies \dot{p}_j = -\dfrac{\partial H}{\partial q_j}$; $\dot{q}_j = \dfrac{\partial H}{\partial p_j}$

❏ Hamilton equations are first order differential equations

❏ $j \to 1 \dots n$ for a system of $n-$degree of freedom.
Thus there are **2n number of first order Hamilton's equations**
$(n - for\ \dot{p}_j\ and\ n - for\ \dot{q}_j)$

❏ **A comparison with Lagrangian**: Lagrange's equations are second order differential equations and the number of equations is n (no. of degrees of freedom)

❏ There is nothing new. Just have rearranged the equations to give momentum much importance than generalized velocity.

❏ **Hamiltonian concept**: Extremely important for quantum mechanics, statistical mechanics.

Conservation of energy from Hamiltonian

$H = H(q_j, p_j, t)$
$$\frac{dH}{dt} = \frac{\partial H}{\partial q_j}\frac{dq_j}{dt} + \frac{\partial H}{\partial p_j}\frac{dp_j}{dt} + \frac{\partial H}{\partial t} = -\dot{p}_j\dot{q}_j + \dot{q}_j\dot{p}_j + \frac{\partial H}{\partial t}$$
$$\frac{dH}{dt} = \frac{\partial H}{\partial t}$$

❏ If Lagrangian does not explicitly contain time, then Hamiltonian must not have explicit time dependence, as
$$\frac{\partial L}{\partial t} = -\frac{\partial H}{\partial t} = 0 = \frac{dH}{dt}; \qquad H = constant \text{ of motion}$$

❏ *Remember, if potential is velocity independent*
$$\sum_j p_j\dot{q}_j = \sum_j \frac{\partial L}{\partial \dot{q}_j}\dot{q}_j = \sum_j \frac{\partial T}{\partial \dot{q}_j}\dot{q}_j = 2T$$
$$Then, H = \sum_j p_j\dot{q}_j - L = 2T - (T - V) = T + V = E$$

❏ *If H does not have explicite time dependence $(\frac{\partial H}{\partial t} = 0)$ and potential is velocity independent, then $H = E = const$*

<u>Tutorial I</u>

1. The position vector of a moving particle at any time, t, is given by
   $\bar{r}(t) = (2t^2 - 3)\hat{i} + (4t + 4)\hat{j} + (t^3 + 2t^2)\hat{k}$. Find (i) the distance of the particle from
   the origin at t=0, (ii) the velocity of the particle at t=1 and (iii) the acceleration of the
   particle at t=2.

2. Show that for a particle of constant mass the kinetic energy T satisfies, $\frac{dT}{dt} = \bar{F}.\bar{v}$ and
   if the mass varies, $\frac{d(mT)}{dt} = \bar{F}.\bar{p}$.

3. Show that the centre of mass $\mathbf{R}$ of a system of particles about an arbitrary origin satisfies,

$$M^2 R^2 = M \sum_i m_i r_i^2 - 1/2 \sum_{i,j} m_i m_j r_{ij}^2$$

   where M is the total mass, $r_{ij} = |\mathbf{r_i} - \mathbf{r_j}|$ and $R = |\mathbf{R}|$.

4. The trajectory of an insect in plane polar coordinates is given by, $r = b\exp(\Omega t)$ and
   $\theta = \Omega t$. Show that the velocity and acceleration of the particle at any instant satisfies,
   $\mathbf{v} = r\Omega(\hat{r} + \hat{\theta})$ and $\mathbf{a} = 2\Omega^2 r\hat{\theta}$. Find the angle between the $\mathbf{v}$ and $\mathbf{a}$.

5. Three atoms located at (0.0,0.0,0.0), (0.0, $2^{1/6}\sigma$, 0.0) and (σ, 0.0, 0.0) interact with
   each other through Lennard-Jones potential,

$$V = 4\epsilon \left(\left(\frac{\sigma}{r_{ij}}\right)^{12} - \left(\frac{\sigma}{r_{ij}}\right)^6 \right).$$

   where $r_{ij} = |\mathbf{r_i} - \mathbf{r_j}|$ and σ is a constant. Find

   (i) an expression for the force between a pair of atoms,

   (ii) calculate the total force on the atom at the origin, and

   (iii) the total potential energy of the system.

Tutorial II

1. Find the degree of freedom of a carbon-dioxide molecule ($O{=}C{=}O$) moving in 3-dimensions under each of the following "models".

    (a) The $C{=}O$ bonds are rigid, and $\angle$O-C-O is rigid and is equal to 180°.

    (b) The $C{=}O$ bonds are harmonic (flexible), but $\angle$O-C-O is rigid and is equal to 180°.

    (c) The $C{=}O$ bonds are rigid, but $\angle$O-C-O is flexible.

    (d) The $C{=}O$ bonds and $\angle$O-C-O are flexible.

2. Find the number of degree's of freedom of a CH_4 molecule according to the following models,

    (a) All C-H bonds and all H-C-H angles ($\angle$H-C-H) are stiff

    (b) All C-H bonds are harmonic but all $\angle$H-C-H are stiff

    (c) All C-H bonds are stiff but all $\angle$H-C-H vary

    (d) All C-H bonds and all $\angle$H-C-H are harmonic

3. Use the D'Alembert's principle of virtual work to obtain the equation of motion of the following 2-D systems:

    (a) a simple pendulum.

    (b) a particle moving in a parabolic ($y = ax^2$) wire under gravity.

    (c) a particle sliding down a wedge of angle α.

Tutorial III

1. Determine (i) the constraint relations and (ii) the degrees of freedom; then (iii) device a set of generalized coordinates, (iv) set up the Lagrangian, and obtain (v) the Lagrange's equations of motion for the following systems:

   (a) double pendulum (treat it as 2-D problem)
   (b) spherical pendulum
   (c) A mass m moves on a parabolic wire $y = c x^2$ under gravity. c is a constant (2-D problem).

2. Two masses m_1 and m_2 connected by a light inextensible string of length l. Mass m_1 moves on a horizontal surface, while mass m_2 moves vertically down under gravity as shown in the figure. Set up the Lagrangian of the system and obtain the Euler-Lagrange equations of motion.

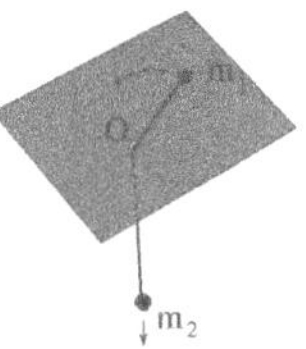

3. Show that if $\mathcal{L}(q, \dot{q}, t)$ is a Lagrangian of a system, $\mathcal{L}'(q, \dot{q}, t) = \mathcal{L}(q, \dot{q}, t) + \frac{dF}{dt}$ is also a valid Lagrangian of the system where $F = F(q, t)$ is a differentiable otherwise arbitrary function.

4. A small block of mass m slides down a wedge of angle θ as shown in the figure. The whole motion is in the X-Y plane. Obtain the Lagrange's equations of motion for the following cases:

   (a) the wedge is stationary.
   (b) the wedge (of mass M) is moving on a horizontal surface due to the reaction of the moving mass m.

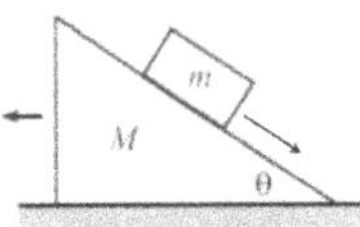

Tutorial IV

Note: Neglect friction unless otherwise stated. You need not have to solve the differential equations unless specifically asked to.

1. Setup the Lagrangian and obtain the Euler-Lagrange equations for the following systems. Obtain the generalized momenta and forces. Determine the number of constants of motion, and try to identify them in each of the cases.

   (a) A pendulum bob of mass m, connected to a point "O" by inextensible string of length l, is oscillating in the $X - Y$ plane. The point of suspension "O" is moving vertically with time as, $O(t) = O_0 + a\,t + b\,t^2$, where a and b are constants.

   (b) A mass m is constrained to move on a parabolic wire ($y = A\,x^2$) under gravity $F = -mg\hat{z}$. The wire is rotated about the z-axis at an angular velocity ω.

   (c) A mass m is constrained to move on the surface of a sphere of radius R under gravity $F = -mg\hat{z}$.

   (d) Two masses m_1 and m_2 are connected by a light inextensible rod of length l. The masses are moving on the $X - Y$ plane such that, the first one is constrained to move on the X-axis while the other on the Y-axis.

2. Using Euler-Lagrange's equations obtain the equation of motion of a stone falling under gravity. The air drag on the stone is given by $\mathbf{F} = -k\mathbf{v}$.

3. A circular hoop of mass M and radius R that *rolls* down (without sliding) an incline under gravity. The angle of the incline with the horizontal is α. Obtain the equation of motion of the hoop using,

   (a) Euler-Lagrange equations for holonomic constraints.

   (b) the method of Lagrange's undetermined multipliers.

4. Show that the geodesics (that is the shortest path between a pair of points on the surface) of,

   (a) a plane is a straight line.

   (b) a cylinder is a helix.

   (c) a sphere is the great circle (the plane of which contain the center of the circle).

Tutorial V

Note: Neglect friction unless otherwise stated. You need not have to solve the differential equations unless specifically asked to.

1. Find the radius of the circular orbit of a particle having mass m and angular momentum l for the following central forces, **(a)** $V(r) = k\,r^2$ and **(b)** $V(r) = k\,r^4$.

2. The orbit of Halleys comet around sun has an eccentricity of 0.967 and a period of 76 years. **(a)** Find the distance of the comet from the sun at perihelion and at aphelion. **(b)** Find the angular velocity of the comet when it is closest to sun. (Useful data: mass of sun$= 2\times10^30$ kg; G$= 6.67 \times 10^{11}$ in S.I. Mass of the comet is negligible when compared to sun.)

3. For circular and parabolic orbits in an attractive K/r potential having the same angular momentum, **(a)** show that the perihelion distance of the parabola is one half the radius of the circle. **(b)** the speed of a particle at any point in a parabolic orbit is $\sqrt{2}$ times the speed in circular orbit passing through the same point.

4. Two particles move about each other in circular orbits under the influence of gravitational force, with a period τ. The motion is suddenly stopped at a given instant of time, and they are then released and allowed to collide each other. Prove that they collide after a time of $\tau/4\sqrt{2}$.

5. Two particles of equal mass, m, interact through gravitational potential. The initial conditions for the system (that is, the position and velocity of one of the particles at time, $t = 0$, relative to the other particle) is given by: $x(0) = 0$, $y(0) = \alpha$, $\dot{x}(0) = -(\frac{3Gm}{\alpha})^{1/2}$ and $\dot{y}(0) = (\frac{Gm}{\alpha})^{1/2}$. Where G is the gravitational constant and α some constant. Determine the shape of the orbit, make a schematic sketch of the same, and obtain the apsidal distances.

Tutorial VI-A

1. Find the Coriolis deflection of a stone dropped from a tower (of height h, and situated at a latitude λ) as it hits the ground. What's the direction of the deflection. Make suitable approximations.

2. A small toy car of mass m moves outward (in a straight line) with uniform speed u_0 from the centre of a turn table. If the turn table takes τ second to complete one rotation, find the forces acting on the car, when it is at a distance r from the centre of the table. What's the velocity of the car at this point for a stationery observer.

3. The trajectory of a particle of mass m on a turn table is $r(t) = \alpha\,t$ and $\theta(t) = \beta\,t$, in polar coordinates. α and β are constants. The turn table rotates about an axis perpendicular to the plane of the table at a uniform angular velocity $\omega\hat{z}$. Find the linear velocity and angular velocity of the particle for an observer in an inertial frame. Find the inertial forces acting on the particle at time t.

   All the quantities should be expressed in terms of $\hat{r}$, $\hat{\theta}$ and $\hat{z}$, where $\hat{r}$ and $\hat{\theta}$ are unit vectors of the plane polar coordinates defined on the table.

4. The structure of a CH_4 molecule may be viewed as: the C sitting at the centre of a cube and H's at alternate corners of the cube. Find the inertia tensor for a CH_4 molecule with the centre of the "enveloping" cube placed at the origin, and axes along three of it's face centres. Mass of H and C-H bond lengths can be taken as unity.

5. Find the inertia tensor for a cone of height h and base radius R, with its apex at the origin and its axis along the z-axis of the coordinate system. Using suitable transformation find the inertia tensor in the coordinate frame with its origin at the centre of mass, but having the same orientation as the original frame.

1. Find (a) the inertia tensor, (b) principal moments of inertia and (c) semi-axes of inertia ellipsoid, for a solid cube of size a and density ρ. The cube has one of its corners at the origin, and three adjacent edges along the axes of the coordinate frame.

   (a) Find the orientation of the principal axes w.r.t the original axes.

   (b) Find the rotation matrix that relate the two sets of axes.

   (c) Find the kinetic energy of the cube if it is rotated with an angular velocity ω (a) about the z-axis (b) about the face diagonal through the origin that lies on the XZ-plane (c) about the body axis though the origin.

2. A solid sphere with its center at the origin of the coordinate axis is cut along XY, YZ and XZ planes into eight equal pieces. Calculate the inertia tensor for the piece in the 1st octant of the coordinate axes $(x \geq 0; y \geq 0; z \geq 0)$. Find the kinetic energy of the solid when rotated about an axis passing through (1, 1, 1) and the origin of the coordinate axes. The density of the sphere is ρ and radius is R.

3. A thin lamina of mass M is in the shape of a 45° right triangle $\mathbf{ABC}$, with $\angle A = 90^\circ$ and sides $AB = AC = l$. Vertex A is at the origin of the coordinate system and vertices B and C lie on the X and Y-axes respectively (see figure).

   (a) Find the inertia tensor of the lamina with respect to the coordinate axes (X, Y, Z).

   (b) Find the inertia tensor of the lamina about a coordinate axes (X', Y', Z'), which is parallel to (X, Y, Z) but with origin at the center of mass of the lamina.

   (c) Find the inertia tensor of the lamina with respect to the (X, Y, Z) axes after being rotated about the Z-axis by an angle 30°.

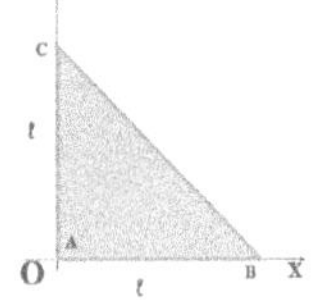

4. A rigid body of mass M and having principal moments, I_1, I_2, I_3 about its centre of mass is suspended by a point on its x_1 axis. The body is set to oscillatory motion in plane perpendicular to the x_3 axis. Find the period of small angle oscillations of the body using Euler equations. Take l as the distance of the point of suspension from the centre of mass. Find the value of l for which the period of oscillation a minimum?

2. A rigid body of mass M and having principal moments, I_1, I_2, I_3 about its centre of mass is suspended by a point on its x_1 axis. The body is set to oscillatory motion in plane perpendicular to the x_3 axis. Find the period of small angle oscillations of the body using Lagrangian method. Take l as the distance of the point of suspension from the centre of mass.

3. Derive the Euler-Lagrange equations for a solid cylinder of mass M and radius a rolling inside a static hollow cylinder of radius R under gravity $(R > a)$. Find the frequency of small oscillations of the centre of mass of the small cylinder.

4. A thin homogeneous disk of mass M and radius r is pivoted to a vertical pole by a light rod of length l passing through the center C of the disk (see figure on right). The disk rolls on the horizontal surface with out slipping such that its center C traces a circle of radius l about the pole at a frequency Ω. The motion of the disk about the pole is in the counter clock-wise direction. Find the kinetic energy of the system. Express the instantaneous angular velocity of the system in cylindrical coordinates.

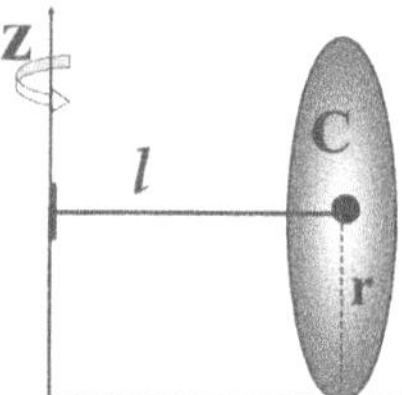

<u>Tutorial VIII</u>

1. Formulate the Hamiltonian and obtain the Hamilton's equations of motion for the following systems:

(a) Two point masses m_1 and m_2 are connected by a light inextensible string of length l and slides on the surface of prism with angles α and β (see figure on right). Gravity acts vertically downward as shown.

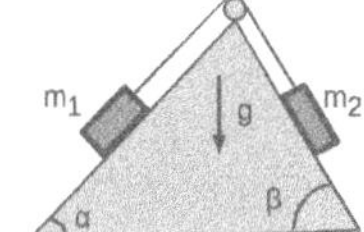

(b) The two body central force with $V = -K/r$. Using the Poisson bracket formalism show that the p_θ is a constant of motion.

(c) Two dimensional motion of a projectile under gravity. Treat in both (a) Cartesian and (b) plane polar coordinates. For case (a) show that p_x is conserved using the Poisson bracket.

(d) An isotropic harmonic oscillator in two dimensions, ie., having equal force constants, $k = m\omega^2$. Show that $A = \frac{1}{2m}(p_x p_y + m^2\omega^2 xy)$ is a constant of motion.

(e) For a point mass m confined to move on the surface of a sphere of radius R under gravity. Identify the constants of motion, with supporting proof using Poisson bracket formalism.

References

1. D. Halliday, R. Resnick, and J. Walker, *Fundamentals of Physics*, Wiley, 2007.

2. R. C. Hibbeler, *Engineering Mechanics: Dynamics*, 14th ed., Pearson, 2015.

3. J. B. Marion and S. T. Thornton, *Classical Dynamics of Particles and Systems*, 5th ed., Brooks/Cole, 2003.

4. J. R. Taylor, *Classical Mechanics*, University Science Books, 2005.

5. D. Kleppner and R. Kolenkow, *An Introduction to Mechanics*, Cambridge University Press, 2011.

6. L. D. Landau and E. M. Lifshitz, *Mechanics (Course of Theoretical Physics, Vol. 1)*, Butterworth-Heinemann, 1976.

7. K. R. Symon, *Mechanics*, 3rd ed., Addison-Wesley, 1971.

8. H. Goldstein, C. P. Poole, and J. L. Safko, *Classical Mechanics*, 3rd ed., Pearson, 2002.

9. P. A. Tipler and G. Mosca, *Physics for Scientists and Engineers*, 6th ed., W. H. Freeman, 2007.

10. D. Morin, *Introduction to Classical Mechanics: With Problems and Solutions*, Cambridge University Press, 2008.